The Marches

40 Town and Country Walks

The author and publisher have made every effort to ensure that the information in this publication is accurate, and accept no responsibility whatsoever for any loss, injury or inconvenience experienced by any person or persons whilst using this book.

published by
pocket mountains ltd
The Old Church, Annanside, Moffat,
Dumfries and Galloway, DG10 9HB
www.pocketmountains.com

ISBN: 978-1-907025-18-1

Text and photography copyright © Ben Giles

The right of Ben Giles to be identified as the Author of this work has been asserted by him in accordance with the Copyright, Designs and Patents Act 1988

A catalogue record for this book is available from the British Library

All route maps are based on 1945 Popular Edition Ordnance Survey material and revised from field surveys by Pocket Mountains Ltd, 2011. © Pocket Mountains Ltd 2011.

Printed in Poland

Introduction

At its fullest extent the Welsh Marches comprises not only all the counties in western England that border with Wales, from Cheshire in the north to Gloucestershire in the south, but also some southern Welsh counties, from Monmouthshire in the east to Pembrokeshire in the west. However, the name is more popularly used to refer to the heart of the border territory of England and Wales – roughly the country lying between, and to the west of, the cities of Shrewsbury and Hereford. It is this smaller area that this guidebook covers. Indeed, the Welsh Marches of Shropshire and Herefordshire have long been true border country. With a complex and fascinating history, there are wooded river valleys, ruined castles, moorland uplands and ancient market towns, making this perfect walking country for those who prefer a gentler pace and time to explore along the way.

Encircling this area of the Marches are two of Britain's great rivers. Rising close to each other in mid-Wales, the River Severn passes to the north through Shrewsbury on its great clockwise arc to its estuary beyond Gloucester, while the Wye heads southwards before taking a more easterly course through Hay-on-Wye towards Hereford and on finally to join the Severn at Chepstow.

It is here also that the lowlands of England rise from the industrialised Midlands to meet the moorland hills of Wales at the former hunting ranges of the Clun, Mortimer and Radnor Forests. Flowing from this higher ground between the Severn and the Wye are the smaller rivers that serve the towns of the Marches – the Clun and Teme for Knighton and Ludlow, the Lugg and Arrow for Presteigne, Kington and Leominster. In addition, just to the south of the River Wye, hidden away in the shadow of the northern escarpment of the Black Mountains, lie the secluded Golden Valley and the headwaters of the River Monnow. It is often said, but no less true for this, that few parts of Britain can match the varied landscape of the Welsh Marches.

About this guide

This guide contains forty circular routes in Shropshire, Herefordshire and Powys, ranging in length from 3km to 16km.

Most of the routes are intended as comfortable walks or strolls – at most requiring half a summer's day to complete, though a good number can be completed in just an hour or two. On some routes the cumulative ascent or the terrain itself may require greater exertion or concentration, but in general the walking is on well-worn paths, lanes and tracks, with plenty of waymarks which should require minimal time and effort for route-finding. The route descriptions concentrate on the salient points of navigation, but do not cover every twist and turn. If in doubt, the obvious path is usually the line to take. In addition, the accompanying sketch maps serve an illustrative purpose and – for the longer, higher or more complex routes – it is recommended that the relevant OS map is carried.

The recommended time for each walk is an estimate based on an average walking speed of 4kmph, with an allowance added in for ascent and the type of ground. However, this will vary significantly, not only for individuals but also given the seasonal effects on paths, especially those crossing fields. It is hoped there is plenty of interest along the routes themselves and it would be possible to spread a short walk over a half day. Conversely, most routes are short enough to attempt two in a day.

Getting around

The main cities and towns of the Welsh Marches are Shrewsbury, Church Stretton, Craven Arms, Knighton, Ludlow, Presteigne, Kington, Leominster, Hay-on-Wye and Hereford. All have regular bus routes, while mainline railways run between Shrewsbury and Hereford and from Craven Arms through Knighton into Mid Wales. An effort has been made to start walks from places which are served by public transport and it would usually be possible to plan the completion of a walk from a town to coincide with train times. However, many of the outlying rural areas are only intermittently served by public bus on both a weekly and seasonal basis. In addition, Shropshire Hills Shuttles run a bus service at weekends and on Bank Holiday Mondays from April to September, with routes starting from Church Stretton and Craven Arms.

However, access by car is the preferred option for many and, while towns cater adequately for parking, this can be a sensitive issue in small villages and hamlets. Pubs and inns can be very accommodating if the intention is to visit before or after a walk, but where parking is outwith designated car parks consideration should be shown for the needs and access of local residents. Further information is available from tourist information centres in the towns listed above.

Countryside access

The Welsh Marches is an area of mixed farming, with arable, dairy and sheep farming all present. At lambing time, farmers request that dogs are kept on leads. The presence of dogs for cows with calves can be problematic and it is not unheard of for cattle to behave in a very protective way. Even without a dog, cows which have recently calved should be left well alone. If in doubt, it is usually advisable and possible to find a short detour to avoid such livestock. Most paths covered in the routes are well-used and well-maintained by local agencies, but in spring and summer especially hedges and undergrowth grow vigorously and nettles, brambles and bracken can infiltrate narrower paths and stile crossings. Since 2000 the Countryside Rights of Way Act has opened up legal access to large areas of uplands and moorland. In addition, some areas of woodland may have local access agreements. However, sensitivity should be shown for grazing livestock and ground-nesting birds. OS maps mark the limit of access land, where open country is shaded in yellow, while on the ground look out for the circular brown discs with the symbol of a walker against a white background.

A future perspective on the landscape

To a group of travellers at the end of the current millennium, looking up from somewhere deep in the linear mega-city stretching the length of the Welsh Marches (though perhaps the name itself will not have survived), there might yet come the visceral urge to walk and gain high ground and cast their gaze to the still-rolling hills glowering below the horizon. Time-travel and technology notwithstanding, as distant from us then as we are now from the Norman Marcher Lords, they might well shudder at how geologically wild the land once was or at the human histories of ancient Celts in their improbable hillforts, or conquering Romans defeated by the land itself, or robber barons lording it in their castles, all these to them fainter marks and ruins hidden in their urban landscape. How to understand the complexities of the Marches' medieval feudal system or the arbitrary political union of the Tudor kings, or the intricate relations between different nations, languages and cultures, at times a source of antagonism for generations yet seemingly co-existent for centuries, or how the first Industrial Revolution petered out here before it could grip these valleys and floodplains and migrated eastwards to a more compliant landscape – all such considerations to them may be too distant to comprehend.

Preferable to them, most likely, will be their own more recent story of the Marches – how the last fields and farms and villages disappeared and valleys and the slopes of hills filled with people, or perhaps how moorland slopes turned more fertile and became subject to planning and the plough, or how wildlife became encased and access became greater, to our minds controlled and confined, but to theirs deftly conserved. Yet, even as they climb Caradoc's weathered tors or sweep up Hergest's ridge or stride along the fingered scarp of the Black Mountains and with aching limbs tread the still-walked paths, should fog on the clearest of winter mornings or a mist on the stillest of summer evenings cover the conurbation below, on reaching the top and looking out above the sea of cloud at the hilltops and ridges, they might, just, despite another millennium of difference and change, manage a quiet smile of satisfaction that the line of the landscape remains.

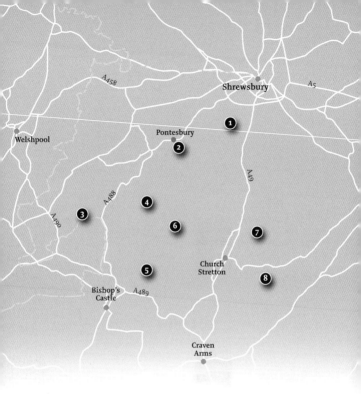

The Church Stretton Hills have long been popular with walkers and tourists, since at least the early 19th century, when easier access by road and rail brought people out of the great conurbations of the Midlands in search of relaxation and cleaner air. Bordered to the west by the Vale of Montgomery, to the north by the city of Shrewsbury and the Cheshire Plain, and to the east by the undulating Midlands, the steep-sided whaleback ridge of the Long Mynd and the rocky tors of Caer Caradoc and the Stiperstones provide opportunities for hillwalking more usually associated with the mountains of Wales and northern England. However, to the east and west lie gentler and lower slopes, especially on the limestone escarpment of Wenlock Edge, while the former spa town of Church Stretton and the surrounding villages more than meet the needs of the modern visitor.

Looking south from Cranberry Rock, Stiperstones ▸

Shrewsbury and the Church Stretton Hills

1 **Lyth Hill Country Park**   8
Keep an eye out for the geology as
well as the views in this popular
country park

2 **Pontesford and Earl's Hill**   10
You'll need a good pair of legs for
this short but challenging route,
but the views are worth it

3 **Stapeley Hill and Mitchell's Fold** 12
Gain your bearings and a sense of
history with views in every direction
from this open hillside

4 **The Stiperstones**   14
This classic Shropshire outing will
not disappoint in any weather

5 **Norbury and Linley Hill**   16
One of Shropshire's less walked
rounds from a secluded village

6 **The Long Mynd and Adstone Hill** 18
Take the longer, western approach
to fully appreciate this famous hill

7 **Caer Caradoc Hill**   20
A bit of puff is needed for the
climb, but the rewards are plentiful
on this classic round

8 **Rushbury and Wenlock Edge**   22
Take your time along this
well-known undulating escarpment

Lyth Hill Country Park

**Distance 3km Time 1 hour
Terrain easy walking, though can be
muddy lower down Map OS Explorer 241
Access bus (544) from Shrewsbury**

**This Countryside Heritage Site south of
Shrewsbury provides a perfect stroll
for all ages.**

Lyth Hill is one of the best spots from
which to view the hills of South
Shropshire. The open grassland on top of
the escarpment combined with the
woodland below gives a varied, if short,
outing, just right for blowing away the
cobwebs on a windy winter's day or a lazy
stroll in summer sun. There are two car
parks on site. The eastern one, 2km south
of Bayston, is more easily accessible and is
the start point for the walk.

Follow the route of the Shropshire Way
through the gate and over the grassland
slope for 600m as it rises gently to the top
of Lyth Hill. Here you'll find the second car

park and a topograph to help interpret the
impressive view, which stretches from the
Wrekin and the line of Wenlock Edge
westwards to the Church Stretton Hills,
and across the gap to the hulk of the Long
Mynd. There is also plenty of birdlife.
Buzzards, kestrels and ravens can often be
seen swooping over the hill. You may even
catch a glimpse of the brightly-coloured
yellowhammer or hear the drilling of a
woodpecker, while on summer evenings
you can watch the acrobatics of swallows
and house martins.

To continue, head along the top of the
escarpment as it starts to descend gently.
The lane on the right is known as Rope
Walk, so called as it was here that hemp
used to be laid out in long lines to be
stretched and then twisted into rope. In
the middle of the 19th century there was
even a windmill to assist in this process,
but the windmill and the days of rope-
making are long gone. The Shropshire

◀ The view from Lyth Hill towards The Wrekin

author Mary Webb also lived nearby, at Spring Cottage, and found the views and surrounding countryside an inspiration for her writings.

On reaching Coppice Gate Cottage keep on the Shropshire Way and pass into the field beyond, with the oak woodland of Spring Coppice on the right – this area of formerly coppiced woodland still has some attractive old oaks, though the name 'spring' probably means 'new', to distinguish it from Old Coppice to the north. After 100m, just after a handy bench, look out for a path which branches sharp left to make a descending traverse through bracken to the bottom of the slope.

At this point, bear left to pass below some wooded crags and a small cliff. Here, it is easy to see the rocks underlying the hill, especially the pebbly conglomerate which often seems like concrete or rubble but, in fact, dates back over 500 million years to the Precambrian period, when some ancient river or flood deposited this mass of rocky material; this was then shaped under huge pressure and subsequently weathered during the intervening millennia into the geological forms visible today.

The route now continues along the bottom of the escarpment and soon passes through a gate and then onto a boardwalk, before making its way alongside a hedge and some houses and onto a lane. Walk along the lane and, at the junction beyond, a left turn up the hill for 250m brings you back to the start.

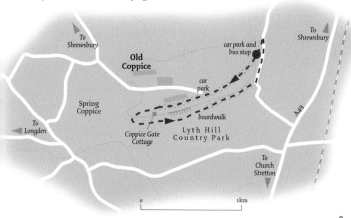

Pontesford and Earl's Hill

**Distance 3.5km Time 1 hour 30
Terrain woodland paths with steep
ascent and descent Map OS Explorer 241
Access bus (552, 553) from Bishop's
Castle, Pontesbury and Shrewsbury
stops at Pontesford Garage on the A488,
600m from the starting point**

**A short walk but not one for the faint-
hearted – a lot of puff is needed for the
ascent of this dragon's back – but the
views are worth it and there's plenty of
wildlife to spot too.**

The 650-million-year-old volcanic slopes
of Pontesford and Earl's Hill tower above
the settlements of Pontesford and
Pontesbury. Local lore has long
maintained the hill is actually a sleeping
dragon – its double humpbacked profile
certainly makes for a fearsome ascent. The
contours also made it an ideal site for the
building of an impressive fort 2500 years
ago during the Iron Age. In more recent
times, the Shropshire author Mary Webb,
who lived at one time in Pontesbury,
popularised another myth associated with
the hill – the legend of the golden arrow –
which holds that whoever finds the arrow,
lost 1400 years ago in a battle between the
kingdoms of Mercia and Wessex, will gain
immense fortune.

For the last half century the area has
been managed by Shropshire Wildlife
Trust and was their first nature reserve,
acquired in 1964, though Pontesford Hill
itself has been leased to the Forestry
Commission, which accounts for its
covering of conifers. The woodlands now
provide a great show of bluebells in the
spring and the numerous nesting boxes
have been set up as encouragement for
migrant birds to breed. The trust has also
recently added 25 acres of meadow on the
hill's eastern side and has long-term plans
to restore its natural habitat to help
maintain the diverse flora and fauna,
which amongst an impressive list counts
29 species of butterfly.

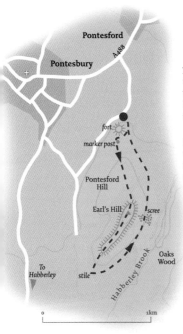

Pontesford

A488

Pontesbury

fort
marker post

Pontesford
Hill

Earl's Hill · · · scree

Habberley Brook · · · Oaks Wood

To Habberley · · · stile

0 · · · 1km

To reach the start of the walk, from the A488 just south of Pontesford village take the minor road (signed Pontesford Hill and Earl's Hill Nature Reserve) for 600m, where there is a parking area tucked away on the left at the edge of the woodland.

Walk out of the rear of the parking area and almost immediately, at a fork, bear to the right, rising uphill for 250m as you circle round and then through the earthworks of the hill's lower Iron Age fort. As the track levels out, look out for a marker post. Here, you'll need to turn left into a conifer plantation and brace yourself for an unremitting ascent of 100m, which can be a little awkward in wet conditions. Pass over the top of Pontesford Hill to a stile on the far side of the plantation.

From here continue ahead up the open grass and bracken-covered slope, dotted with oak and hawthorn, to the triangulation pillar which marks the top of Earl's Hill and gives a commanding view of the Shropshire Hills. You also get a bird's eye view of the town of Pontesbury and it's worth keeping a look-out for peregrines that are known to nest on the hill's eastern crags. The descent follows the grassy southwestern ridge and passes through the hill's higher earthworks. Lower down the path becomes looser and steep enough for care to be needed, but after 600m you reach a stile at the limit of the open hillside.

Just beyond the stile, turn left onto a bridleway. The route now contours the southern and eastern side of the hill on an undulating path, initially alongside open fields on the right with good views to Oaks Wood across Habberley Brook (you can follow a detour down through the nature reserve on paths signed by Shropshire Wildlife Trust) and then into full woodland, where you cross a small scree slope below cliffs to reach the northern end of the reserve. From here you descend across two fields before entering the woodland once again, where the bridleway broadens to a track and leads you back in 500m to the parking area.

◀ On the southwestern ridge of Earl's Hill

Stapeley Hill and Mitchell's Fold

Distance 4km Time 1 hour
Terrain tracks and open hillside
Map OS Explorer 216 Access bus (745)
from Ludlow, (775) Newtown or (553)
Bishop's Castle, with extra 2.5km walk

Step back in time and explore the landscape of one of the most dramatic stone circles in Shropshire.

From the A488 halfway between Bishop's Castle and Minsterley, follow the signs for Mitchell's Fold Stone Circle for 2km along the minor road through the settlement of White Grit along the northern side of Corndon Hill, before turning right down a rough track for 350m to a parking area. (To access by bus from the A488, walk down the same minor road towards White Grit, but leave it after 500m to continue ahead on a track for another 500m and join the route at the base of Stapeley Hill's southern ridge.)

Leave the far end of the parking area on a grassy track over the bracken-covered hillside to reach the stone circle of Mitchell's Fold after 300m. No-one quite knows what the purpose of the circle was. Even the number of stones is in dispute and there is a possible cairn of unknown significance on top of the rise a little to the southeast. The tallest stone itself may have been one of a pair marking the entrance to the circle. At any rate the current stones date to the Bronze Age, when nearby Corndon Hill was also a source of igneous stone for axe-heads. Whatever the origins, the location is still impressive, especially the view westwards

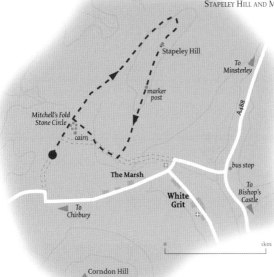

To Minsterley

Stapeley Hill

marker post

A488

Mitchell's Fold
Stone Circle

cairn

bus stop

The Marsh

To
Bishop's
Castle

White
Grit

To
Chirbury

0   1km

Corndon Hill

to the skyline, where you can pick out the hill ranges of Plunlumon, Cadair Idris, the Arans, Arenigs and the Berwyns – an encompassing view, particularly when silhouetted by the setting sun.

To continue, stroll along the track that heads northeastwards, with the cairn on top of Stapeley Hill clearly visible ahead. After 1km, or a little more if you wish, you can branch off the main track and make your way over the moorland along one of the many sheep trods and up to the cairn that tops the slim ridge of Stapeley Hill. If possible, this gives an even better viewpoint than the stone circle, especially eastwards to Stiperstones and southwards to the hulk of Corndon Hill.

Between these hills is the Pontesford-Linley geological faultline. Lying on a northeast-southwest axis, this fault runs in a similar direction to its better known cousin, the Church Stretton Fault, on the eastern side of the Long Mynd.

The return follows the hill's southern ridge, initially broad, but once over a crosspaths (ignore the marker post) the sides steepen and the crest becomes surprisingly well-defined, with a small valley on the right and rocky outcrops to the left. Once you reach the base of the ridge, by a wall and fence, turn right onto a track (or left to return to the bus stop). This takes you uphill for 200m and down across a stream before a final pull up onto the open moorland to return to the stone circle and the track to the parking area.

◀ Stapeley Hill from Mitchell's Fold Stone Circle

13

The Stiperstones

**Distance 5.5km Time 2 hours
Terrain moorland paths, rocks and
boulders Map OS Explorer 216 or 217
Access Shropshire Hills Shuttle bus (April
to September, limited service)**

**Stride or scramble along this well-known
ridge of rocky tors – ideal for a quick
outing or take your time and explore
every nook and cranny.**

The walk starts from the Stiperstones
Nature Reserve car park just above The
Bog Visitor Centre. The most
straightforward approach by car is from
the A488 to the west, where a well-signed
but narrow road heads up through Shelve
and Pennerley. From the east a high
moorland road rises from the settlement
of Bridges, north of Wentnor. The
Shropshire Shuttle Bus runs a seasonal
service, though only on weekends and
Bank Holiday Mondays. The Bog Visitor
Centre, a former schoolhouse, is well
worth a visit.

From the top of the car park above the
visitor centre a narrow path (signed
Shropshire Way 500m) climbs
uphill, past a pond and

up through bracken and scrub, then
over a rough pasture to a gate. Set out
across the field beyond and then bear left
to pick up the line of the Shropshire Way,
which runs along the top of this broad
section of ridge.

This well-worn route takes you across
the moorland road from Bridges and onto
a rocky and peaty path up through the
heather. After 500m you reach Cranberry
Rock, the first in a series of jagged tors
which are all that is left of rocks that
started life about 500 million years ago as
a white sandy beach in the southern
hemisphere. The softer sandstone has
been eroded by millennia of ice, wind,
rain and sun to leave the fissured shapes
we see today. The name Stiperstone itself
is thought to mean 'stripped stone',
reflecting the frost-shattered appearance
of the light-coloured but harder quartzite
that remains. A traverse of the tors gives

Stiperstones

some enticing, if in places rather loose, options for impromptu scrambling, though a straightforward path on their right means you can avoid the use of your hands. The second main outcrop is Mainstone Rock, topped by a triangulation point which marks the high point of the ridge. There are plenty of niches here to shelter from the weather or admire the views – to the east is the squat bulk of the Long Mynd, the Cheshire Plain stretches away to the north, and on a clear day you can see the Clun Forest rolling away to the south, while to the west rise the peaks of Snowdonia.

The third main outcrop on the ridge is the Devil's Chair, and, as you would expect, there is a legend behind the name. Local lore has it that the Devil rested here on his way to dam the River Severn; on standing up he caused all the boulders now lying around to spill out from his seat. If the geologist in you makes you sceptical, perhaps you'll still want to avoid coming here on 22 December each year, when all the ghosts in the area are reputed to meet at this satanic spot. And if this does not put you off, consider the strange tale of the Seven Whistlers – if you see six birds searching the moorland here for their lost companion, pray they

don't find their friend. Their reunion will signify the end of the world. Eschatological matters aside, the route now continues for 500m down to a small cairn at a crosspaths.

Here, a left turn leads downhill over the moorland for 1.1km to a gate a little way up from a house. Head left along the wide track, which contours the hillside for 1km and passes through three gates, at the third one crossing the Black Ditch, which may date back to medieval times and was part of a field drainage system. The track now descends to the road, which in another 200m leads you back down to the car park and visitor centre.

◀ Mainstone Rock, Stiperstones

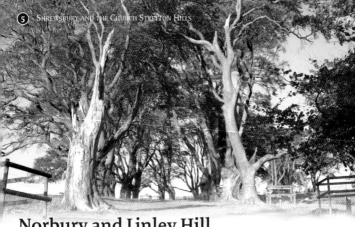

Norbury and Linley Hill

Distance 7.5km Time 2 hours 15
Terrain lanes, fields Map OS Explorer 216
Access no bus service

Wind your way up a quiet lane before climbing the open high ground above Norbury and down the picturesque line of the Linley Beeches.

The village of Norbury lies to the north of the A489 on the higher ground between the valleys of the West and East Onny rivers, 6km northeast of Bishop's Castle. The centre of the village is clustered around the pub, the Sun Inn, and the Church of All Saints, known for its painted vaulted ceiling, ornate altar reredos and rood screen, and its ancient yew tree.

The walk starts along the tree-lined lane on the north side of the churchyard. Follow the lane for 1.2km, initially heading down and then gently up alongside a stream, before a steeper section winds its way through two S-bends. At the second bend look out for a fingerpost for a bridleway off to the left. This route leads you off through a gateway and along a fence and soon curves to the right as it climbs northwards on a grassy track up over four fields to the top of the rise. If you need an excuse to pause and catch your breath, there is an increasingly impressive view to the Long Mynd to the east, the Stiperstones to the north and westwards to the prominent whaleback of Corndon Hill.

As the gradient eases you can also see the route ahead along the undulating ridge. A handy fenceline shows the way for the next 1km as you initially descend across a wide, shallow dip before heading up over another broad top. Here, keeping to the fence avoids the worst of a marshy area at the head of the small valley on the left. At a gate in a right-angle of fences you should bear left across the grassy

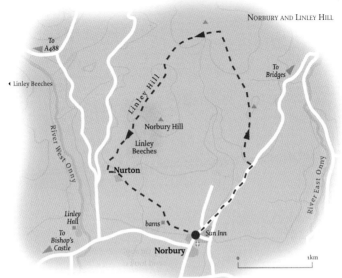

pasture of two fields as you curve around the top of the valley to a small stand of beech trees.

Now heading southwestwards, a descent for 500m, down and across a dip, soon brings you up to a stile on the Shropshire Way. Here, a left turn onto this waymarked route for the next 1.5km leads up over a grassy shoulder and then down to the start of an avenue of planted beech trees which act as a picturesque guide down the southwest ridge of the hill. These beech trees are thought to have been planted in the middle of the 18th century by the area's then Member of Parliament, Robert More. He not only had Linley Hall built at the bottom of the ridge but, as a Fellow of the Royal Society and friend of the botanist Linnaeus, he also set about creating an impressive

park. The approach to the Hall itself lay along what became a mile-long avenue of oaks, while on the slopes above he laid out his double line of beech trees – all the more impressive to his guests for their exposed and elevated position.

At the end of the avenue, just beyond a stile, you'll need to leave the line of the ridge and turn left over a second stile onto a grassy track past the cottage and farm buildings at Nurton. Some 50m beyond the barns, fork left over fields in a southeasterly direction – head diagonally down the first field to a footbridge over the stream, climb up the rise in the second field and then bear slightly to the right down the third field to a cluster of barns. From this point, a track bears off left and soon becomes a hedged lane to take you back down into Norbury.

The Long Mynd and Adstone Hill

Distance 16km Time 5 hours
Terrain lanes, fields and high moorland
tracks Map OS Explorer 217
Access Shropshire Hills Shuttle bus (April
to September, limited service)

A walk full of contrasts, from the small but
shapely ridge of Adstone Hill to the open
moorland slopes of the Long Mynd and the
secluded and tranquil Darnford Valley.

This walk starts from the settlement of
Bridges near the village of Ratlinghope at
the head of the East Onny Valley above
Wentnor. There is parking available on the
roadside or in the car park of the former
Horseshoe Inn. It is worth noting that the
high route along the Long Mynd is clear
enough in good weather, though in poor
visibility good map-reading skills and use
of a compass may be essential.

The first part of the walk follows the
Shropshire Way to Adstone. Set off along
the lane past the former inn and over the
Darnford Brook, which meets the River East

Onny here. The lane starts to climb – in
500m, at a left-hand bend, take the footpath
off to the right and then in another 30m, at
a gateway, fork left off the track.

Now heading up the north ridge of
Adstone Hill, the route offers great views
of the Stiperstones and the Long Mynd
itself. From the top descend the far side to
the road, where a left turn takes you down
through the settlement of Adstone. At the
sharp right bend you now leave the
Shropshire Way and go straight ahead
down a rough, tree-lined byway, across the
stream at the bottom and up to the
buildings of Medlicott. At the lane junction
beyond, keep ahead up the increasingly
steep gradient to the start of the open
hillside and Medlicott Cottage.

The gradient eases as the track enters
National Trust land and starts to wind its
way for the next 1km around the flanks of
Pole Bank and up to a crosspaths on top of
the Long Mynd's broad ridge. Here, you can
detour right to the top of Pole Bank, where

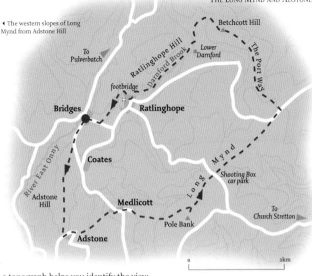

◄ The western slopes of Long Mynd from Adstone Hill

a topograph helps you identify the view and contemplate the expanse of this 'Long Mountain' which contains more than 25 Bronze Age burial mounds. The onward route rejoins the Shropshire Way and bears northeastwards along the ridge – in 800m crossing the road rising from the Cardingmill Valley at the Shooting Box car park and then in another 1.7km meeting the moorland road between Ratlinghope and Woolstaston. Walk along this road for 200m and then turn left, with the Shropshire Way, onto the Port Way.

This ancient trackway is your guide for the next 2.5km as it descends across a stream and then leads northwards over some small rises, before veering to the left across the low point above Upper Darnford and up to the top of Betchcott Hill. From

here, the Port Way descends into a dip, where you should keep on the Shropshire Way as it turns left and drops down into the steep-sided valley.

The path down through the bracken can be rather boggy, but once across the Darnford Brook it follows a drier line a little above its northern bank and in 1.5km brings you opposite the village of Ratlinghope. Here, it is well worth a detour across the stream and right to see the delightful church.

From Ratlinghope you can recross the brook a little further down, where the gentle onward route continues for 1km along the now wooded northern bank to the road. Here, a right turn takes you back to Bridges.

Caer Caradoc Hill

**Distance 6.5km Time 2 hours 30
Terrain lanes, field paths, steep bracken
and grass slopes Map OS Explorer 217
Access bus (435, 540) from Ludlow,
Church Stretton and Shrewsbury or (780)
from Church Stretton**

**Cross the area's most famous geological
faultline and a legendary Romano-British
battleline in an airy climb up one of
Shropshire's best ridges.**

Just to the north of the town and former
Victorian spa of Church Stretton, along the
B5477, is the small village of All Stretton.
There is some roadside parking near the
Yew Tree pub, or, with permission, walkers
are able to use the rear of its large car park.
Many walkers use the access to the Batch
Valley to ascend the Long Mynd, but this
walk takes you across the geological line
of the Church Stretton Fault and up the
steep slopes of Caer Caradoc, from where,
standing on the hill's volcanic rocks you
can look back westwards to the smoother
sedimentary rocks that largely make up
the Long Mynd.

Walk down the road towards Church
Stretton past the lane leading to the
village hall and in 50m turn left down
Farm Lane – the first house on the right,
Essex Lodge, has a traditional timber-
framed panel preserved behind some
perspex. As the lane takes you down
through the heart of the pretty village,
bear left at a junction and on over a
stream and then the railway to the A49
main road, with the bulk of Caer Caradoc
Hill ahead.

Across the road, a field path follows the
left-hand fence beside an old hollow-way
to rise gently up over three fields, with the
buildings and ponds of New House Farm
away to the right. At the top of the third
field cross the fence and continue climbing
up into the narrowing valley. Two gates
lead the way into some woodland
alongside an alder-lined stream, where you
may be joined on the right by walkers from
Church Stretton. The route here levels out,

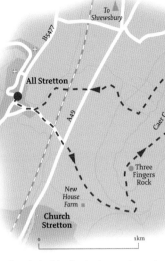

To Shrewsbury

B5477

Little Caradoc

All Stretton

A49

Caer Caradoc Hill

Caer Caradoc Fort

Three Fingers Rock

New House Farm

Church Stretton

0   1km

stand' against the occupying Romans in AD50. If Caer Caradoc truly is where the Romans defeated Caratacus and the Ordovices tribe, it must mark the place the defeated men fled – not even Romans could fight their way up these slopes.

To descend, follow the north ridge steeply down into the dip ahead and, where the fence comes in from the right just past a small outcrop of rock but before a small pool, bear sharp left to pick up the start of a path which makes a delightful descending traverse down to a fence and hedge. Here, bear left for 600m onto an undulating path that contours the hill's northern slope, passing through some thin deciduous woodland of ash and hawthorn and over a series of re-entrants with side-streams issuing from springs further up the hillside.

Just beyond the third re-entrant look out for a path off to the right, which descends over two fields alongside the fence and stream to a gate into woodland. A track now takes you down through the stand of trees and across a field to the A49. Cross the road and on the far side of the field beyond you'll need to negotiate the unmanned railway crossing. Now head diagonally left to a stile and then right onto an old tree-lined lane, finally bearing left to follow the stream for 250m to return to the lower end of All Stretton and the outward route.

though don't be deceived as 50m beyond a small footbridge across the stream look out for a path rising to the left. You'll need to brace yourself for a short but unremittingly steep ascent of 125m to Three Fingers Rock, the first of the ancient volcanic crags along Caer Caradoc's southern ridge.

From here, the going along the grassy ridge is gentler for the next 1km, though you are fully exposed to any weather thrown at you. However, on a clear day you have plenty of time to take in the views westwards to the Long Mynd, eastwards to Hope Bowdler Hill and ahead to Shrewsbury and the Cheshire Plain. The final rise to the craggy top passes through the earthworks of the hill's Iron Age hillfort.

The hill has long been associated with the Celtic chieftain Caratacus and his 'last

◀ Approaching the top of Caer Caradoc

Rushbury and Wenlock Edge

Distance 6km Time 1 hour 45
Terrain lanes, fields and woodland
Map OS Explorer 217 Access limited bus
service (540) from Shrewsbury and
Cardington or (155) from Ludlow and
Cardington to Wall under Heywood on the
B4371, 1km north of the start

**Climb over fields and through woods to
Wenlock Edge for views from Shropshire's
longest escarpment.**

To some the name of Wenlock Edge may
perhaps immediately conjure up learning
by heart at school the opening lines of A E
Housman's poem 'On Wenlock Edge the
wood's in trouble'. Housman, in his all too
melancholic way, imagined how an
unbroken series of long-perished
observers from Roman times 'At yonder
heaving hill would stare', heaving because
'The gale, it plies the saplings double'. And
Wenlock Edge truly does catch the wind, its
long escarpment stretching
northeastwards from Craven Arms to
Much Wenlock and on to Ironbridge.

Take the B4371 from Church Stretton
through the village of Hope Bowdler to
Wall under Heywood. From here, turn off
to Rushbury, where there is some roadside
parking near the church and school. The
village of Rushbury lies at the foot of
Wenlock Edge in the valley of Apedale and
though small it has a considerable history.
It grew up as a settlement at the meeting
of two Roman roads, one of which crosses
Wenlock Edge at Roman Bank. St Peter's
Church, though dating from the 13th
century, has some Saxon herring-bone
masonry on its northern and southern
outer walls, while the half-timbered and
yellow-panelled Manor House at the
northern edge of the village dates to
Elizabethan times. A plaque on the outside
of the school records the bequest of
Benjamin Wainwright in 1821 and Victorian
daytrippers came here by tram and rail to
the old station.

From the church, walk along the lane
past the school and bear left for 100m
down the hill. Just before the stream a

◄ Old oak pollard below Wenlock Edge

bridleway leads off right to a delightful packhorse bridge and up to a narrow lane (if this section is muddy or overgrown it may be best to retreat from the bridge and bypass this section on the lanes). Bear right onto the lane, which soon becomes a track and then a bridleway over the line of a disused railway to a large field.

The route from here heads diagonally right over a series of fields on a rising traverse towards Stars Coppice on the skyline – in the second field it's worth a detour to admire the stag-headed oak pollard up on the left and the view back to Hope Bowdler Hill and the Long Mynd. In the third field the path switches to the right of the hedge, up through some thin deciduous woodland to a forestry gate. Beyond, the route climbs steeply to the top end of the plantation to another gate on the broad upper section of Wenlock Edge.

Now bear left up along the field edge and woodland for 200m to pick up the line of the Jack Mytton Way for the next 1.25km. This bridleway passes through old coppiced woodland along the top of Wenlock Edge, with good views right to the masts on Brown Clee Hill and the radar stations on Titterstone Clee Hill, before descending past some cottages and on to the road, Roman in origin, that traverses the ridge between Rushbury and Millichope.

Turn left along the road to the bend and head straight across onto the Shropshire Way (SP Rays Farm) up past some houses and stables into Roman Bank woodland reserve, which is now managed by the National Trust. Once the path begins to descend, look out in 200m for a marker-post and a footpath off to the left. The route now descends on a clear track to the bottom of the wood and then heads down over a series of fields – go diagonally left in the first field, across the bottom corner of the second, over the disused railway line and across the third field to a hedge which guides you back over a stream into a fourth field and on towards the houses and the circular Norman motte of Rushbury.

23

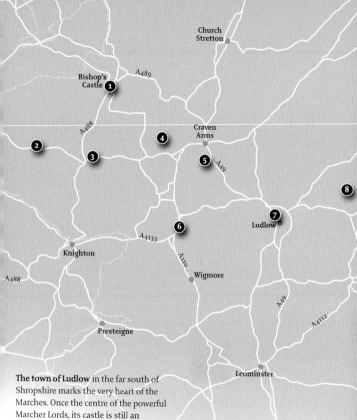

The town of Ludlow in the far south of Shropshire marks the very heart of the Marches. Once the centre of the powerful Marcher Lords, its castle is still an impressive sight and the town itself is busy with locals and tourists alike. To the east across the River Corve lie the Clee Hills, while the Teme and Clun Valleys take you westwards beyond the towns of Leintwardine and Craven Arms to the higher ground of Clun and Bishop's Castle. Further still lies the remote moorland of the Clun Forest and the border with Wales. It's easy to lose oneself in the area's maze of small valleys and undulating hills and for those seeking solitary walking you don't have to go far to lose the crowds, though west of Clun you may meet a string of long-distance walkers on Offa's Dyke Path.

Above Overton looking towards Titterstone Clee Hill ▶

Ludlow and the Clun Forest

1 **Bishop's Castle**   26
An ancient town, riverside meadows and woodland make this a short but satisfying outing

2 **Newcastle and Llanfair Hill**   28
Let Offa's Dyke show you the way high above the Clun Valley

3 **Clun and Bury Ditches**   30
Once you've had your fill of castle and hillfort, leave time to explore this medieval town

4 **Hopesay Hill**   32
Solitude is almost guaranteed on this short round of rolling hills

5 **Craven Arms and Stokesay Castle**   34
A walk of contrasts, from busy town and historic manor house to quiet woodland and open fields

6 **Leintwardine and Downton Hill**   36
Follow in the footsteps of Roman legionaries before taking to higher ground

7 **Ludlow and Mary Knoll Valley**   38
You'll need plenty of time to explore the history and the landscape around this popular Marches town

8 **Titterstone Clee Hill**   40
Gain a sense of perspective as you walk through 5000 years of human impact on the landscape

Bishop's Castle

**Distance 5km Time 1 hour 15
Terrain lanes, fields and woodland
Map OS Explorer 216 Access bus (553)
from Shrewsbury or the Secret Hills
Shuttle bus (April to September,
limited service)**

**Enjoy the sense of history and nature on
this short walk from one of England's
oldest market towns.**

The walk starts from the Market Square
at the top end of Bishop's Castle, where
what remains of the town's Norman
castle now lies in the grounds of the
Castle Hotel. The days when the Bishops
of Hereford exercised their control over
this area have long gone. However, it is
worth pausing in the square to look at the
stone plaque carrying the arms of the Clive
family. A rampant griffin and lion with an
elephant's head recalls Robert Clive's
exploits in India. From the Square, head
down the steep High Street, along which
you can still trace the outlines of the old
burgage plots, past the overhanging House
on Crutches and the town's pubs to the
Church of St John the Baptist at the
bottom end of the town. Of the Norman
building, only the base of the tower
remains, but it is easy to see that it would
have been well-guarded by the castle.

A dogleg right onto Kerry Lane, then
left takes you along Church Lane and past
the fire station. Just beyond this, turn
right onto the route of the Shropshire
Way up Field Lane, which climbs gradually
past some houses towards the top of the
rise. The path now heads over a stile and
continues on a hedge-lined way between
fields for 250m, with good views left to
the Long Mynd. Ignoring any farm tracks
branching off to the left or right, carry on
in the same direction, descending gently
for the next 500m along the bottom edge
of three fields with Bryn Hill and
Blakeridge Wood on the horizon across
the Colebatch Valley.

As you descend more earnestly into the

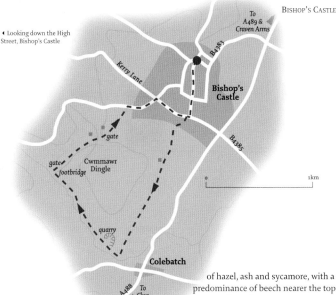

◀ Looking down the High Street, Bishop's Castle

of hazel, ash and sycamore, with a predominance of beech nearer the top edge, to another stile.

In the field beyond, take care to bear left across a small dip and into a second field. Ignore a path off to the right and continue along the left-hand edge of this long narrow field to the top of the rise, from which point you can see the houses of Bishop's Castle, and down to the far end. A gate now marks the way across a smaller field to the start of a track, which in 200m meets Woodbatch Road. A right turn now leads down to a junction with the sunken Kerry Lane, one of the most important of the ancient drovers' roads from Wales into England. Here, to avoid any traffic, bear right past houses along the raised Kerry Green back to the lower end of Bishop's Castle.

valley, in the fourth field you pass a small quarry on the right. Just before the stream the footpath turns right and heads up the secluded Colebatch Valley over a series of sheep-pastured fields beside the tree-lined stream. Once you have crossed a small bridge into the fourth meadow, you'll need to turn right, away from the stream and up the hedgeline towards the wooded dell ahead.

A stile leads into the shaded Cwmmawr Dingle and in 150m a footbridge crosses the small stream, switching you to the opposite bank. From here, the path steepens considerably as it makes a rising traverse up through the mixed woodland

Newcastle and Llanfair Hill

Distance 8km **Time** 2 hours 30 (3 hours with extension) **Terrain** lanes and waymarked paths **Map** OS Explorer 201 **Access** bus (773) from Newtown or Bishop's Castle (very limited service)

Stride out down the Clun Valley before climbing alongside some of the best-preserved parts of Offa's Dyke for far-reaching views over the Clun Forest.

The village of Newcastle lies in the Clun Valley, 6km west of the town of Clun. At whatever time of year you visit, there is a feeling of seclusion. Of course, this valley was once more heavily populated, not least by farm workers, but it is still a thriving village with a school, a pub, The Crown Inn, and a community centre.

Walk up Mill Road to the junction with Church Road and turn right along Church Road for 500m. This pleasant hedged lane, with good views southwards to Spoad Hill and down the Clun Valley, leads to St John's Church, which is notable for its hammerbeam roof and unusual pale pine pews. Continue around the bend, past a road on the left and, 100m further up the hill, look out for a marker post which directs you along Offa's Dyke Path (ODP) on the right. The route descends a field to a footbridge across the River Clun, over the meadows beyond and up to the B4368.

Here, a dogleg left for 30m and then right takes you up through the buildings of Lower Spoad Farm to a tree-lined track up the northern slope of Spoad Hill. It's an ascent of 180m over 1.2km to the road along the ridge, but the gradient is steady as you climb between fields, beside and then across a stream at a double bend. Here, take care to fork right to continue up beside a well-preserved section of Offa's Dyke itself, passing above a cottage down in the dell to the right. Whatever

the true purpose of King Offa's 8th-century earthwork, be it defensive, symbolic, a frontier marker for his kingdom of Mercia, or perhaps all of these, the section from here to Llanfair Hill is truly impressive, even after so many centuries, and somewhat puts into perspective the effort required to construct the dyke.

At the road, turn right past Springhill Farm to the crossroads, where you bear left with ODP and descend for 750m down the narrow lane, with good views of the line of Offa's Dyke as it snakes southwards over Llanfair Hill. The lane swings right and crosses a dip before climbing once more to a triangular area of bracken and trees at the high point. On the southern edge is the grassy mound of a tumulus and some long views over the rolling hills of the Clun Forest, in good weather the perfect spot for a picnic. The northern top of Llanfair Hill is away to the left, on private ground, and, if the urge takes you, it's a straightforward matter to make the high-level stroll for another 1.25km along ODP to the triangulation point at Llanfair Hill's southern end.

The onward route takes the fenced byway northwestwards for 1.6km up over the moorland and down to the road from Spoad Hill. Here, bear left for 50m to the crossroads, where a right turn takes you downhill for 1.5km on a steep but pleasant lane, with intermittent views back across the Clun Valley. At the junction with the B4368, a left turn along the road over the River Clun leads you back past the old mill buildings to the edge of Newcastle village.

◄ Offa's Dyke snaking round Llanfair Hill

29

Clun and Bury Ditches

**Distance 11km Time 3 hours 15
Terrain lanes, tracks and woodland paths
with one steep section Maps OS Explorer
201 and 216 Access bus (773) or Secret
Hills Shuttle from Craven Arms (April to
September, limited service)**

**A sense of history and varied countryside
combine to make this one of the best
walks the Marches has to offer.**

Clun has the appearance of a village, but
it is still heralded as a market town, and
one with a substantial history. The most
obvious features of its past are the
Norman castle and the 15th-century
bridge, originally built for packhorses. Yet
a wander around soon reveals a wealth of
other buildings and it's easy to miss the
original Saxon settlement around St
George's Church to the south of the river.

This walk starts from Clun's small car
park by the castle and roadbridge over the
River Clun. Cross the footbridge over the
river to the rear of the car park and turn
right to explore the castle ruins. The
original castle was built by the Norman de
Say family before passing into the hands of
the Fitzalans, who remodelled the Norman
design into what we can see today, though
it seems to have been somewhat neglected

as early as the end of the 13th century
while the family, as Earls of Arundel,
directed their efforts and money at
Arundel Castle in Sussex.

To continue, bear right in front of Clun
Bowling Club onto the Shropshire Way
which heads down the lane to Castle
Street. A dogleg left for 30m along the road
then right leads to a path between houses,
past a children's play area and through the
memorial hall car park to Mill Lane.

A left turn along this twisting narrow
lane takes you for 1.5km past the youth
hostel, an old mill and then uphill to the
buildings of Guilden Down. Bear right
along the track for 200m to a house with a
bridleway off to the left. This tree-lined
track takes you uphill, through a barrier
and over a rise to a gate at the edge of the
plantations which now surround
Bury Ditches.

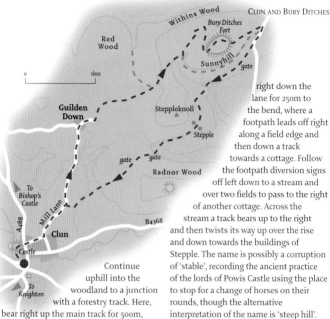

right down the lane for 250m to the bend, where a footpath leads off right along a field edge and then down a track towards a cottage. Follow the footpath diversion signs off left down to a stream and over two fields to pass to the right of another cottage. Across the stream a track bears up to the right and then twists its way up over the rise and down towards the buildings of Stepple. The name is possibly a corruption of 'stable', recording the ancient practice of the lords of Powis Castle using the place to stop for a change of horses on their rounds, though the alternative interpretation of the name is 'steep hill'.

Bear right past the impressive farmhouse down the track for 500m, on the line of the old road between Bishop's Castle and Clun, and pick up a bridleway that descends left across the valley and up to the woodland, before bearing right to the top of the field. Here, dogleg left through a gate then right up through the woodland for 150m, where a right turn at a junction with a permissive path leads to a second gate back into fields. The bridleway now descends for 1km along field edges and then as a sunken lane, veering right to reach Mill Lane, where a left turn takes you onto the outward route back to Clun.

Continue uphill into the woodland to a junction with a forestry track. Here, bear right up the main track for 500m, ignoring other side-tracks, to a crosspaths at the sharp right-hand bend in the track. Take the narrow path off left, steeply up into woodland along a re-entrant for 300m. At the top, dogleg left for 50m, then right for 150m along the track to the top of the rise. Here, again turn right onto a path which contours around the south side of Bury Ditches. In 300m, as the path bends to the left, look out for a gate on the left which leads you up through the earthworks and over the top of the hillfort of Bury Ditches, with its topograph to help interpret the panoramic view.

The route continues down the eastern side of the hill to a car park. Here, turn

◀ Looking west from the ruins of Clun Castle

Hopesay Hill

Distance 5km Time 1 hour 30
Terrain lanes, field paths and tracks with
one fairly steep ascent Map OS Explorer 217
Access Secret Hills Shuttle from Craven
Arms (April to September, limited service)

Take your time on this short but varied
walk from the secluded village of Hopesay
to hilltop views of South Shropshire.

The walk starts from the village of
Hopesay, 1.5km north of Aston on Clun
and the B4368 from Craven Arms. There is
parking available on the road running
through the village. The name Hopesay
echoes both its setting and its history,
'hope' deriving from the Anglo-Saxon
word for an enclosed valley and the second
half of the name recalling that these lands
were in Norman times owned by the de
Say family. The church of St Mary is worth
a detour – it still has a Norman south
doorway and its churchyard is a haven for
wildflowers and grasses.

In the middle of the village, above the
track to the church, pick up signs for the
Shropshire Way and head northwards
towards Edgton, before turning right along
the road to Round Oak. At a bend after
200m, the Shropshire Way takes you down
a lane to the right, past Brookside Cottage,
to a bend – here, keep right up a grassy
track to a gate and the start of Access Land.

Now you start the climb in earnest up
Hopesay Hill. Head up and over a
crosspath, before bearing to the left and
readying yourself for the rising traverse up

the bracken-covered slopes. The hill is steep enough to pace oneself, but after 500m the gradient starts to ease and the path brings you up to the fence at a low point on top of the broad ridge. The southern top of Hopesay Hill lies a 200m detour away to the right, and gives a commanding view of the surrounding area.

The onward route from the low point bears north up alongside the fence, with an increasingly good view to the Long Mynd and, to its left, the Stiperstones, while to the right you can see Caer Caradoc Hill. The path passes just to the left of the highest point of the ridge, before descending for 500m to

the road, with the prominent conifered knoll of Wart Hill beyond.

Turn left to walk for 350m down the road and round the south side of Wart Hill to a junction, where a narrow lane (SP Fish and Hopesay) cuts back down to the left. This pleasant, tree-lined lane wends its way downhill for the next 1.5km and passes through the small settlement of Fish, a name which comes from an alehouse that used to be here, before rejoining the outward route back into Hopesay.

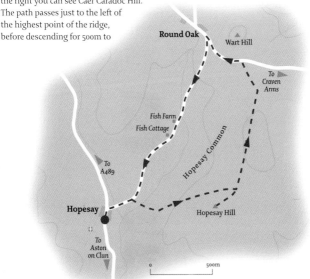

Craven Arms and Stokesay Castle

**Distance 6km Time 1 hour 45
Terrain lanes, woodland tracks and field
paths Map OS Explorer 217 Access train
from Shrewsbury or Hereford, bus (435)
from Shrewsbury and Ludlow, or Secret
Hills Shuttle bus (April to September,
limited service)**

**Stride out on a pleasant stroll over fields
and through woodland with the option to
include a visit to one of the best historic
houses in the Marches.**

The walk starts from the Shropshire
Hills Discovery Centre on the southern
edge of Craven Arms. There is plenty of
parking available and the centre has an
information hall and a café. The modern-
looking design of the centre, while not to
all tastes, is very much in keeping with the
history of Craven Arms. The grid pattern of
the town hints at its history. The coming
of the railways in the 19th century turned
the village into a planned town and it
became an important junction for those

travelling by train between Shrewsbury
and Hereford or from the Midlands into
Wales. The trains still run and the town
continues to grow.

Head to the rear of the centre and follow
the signs onto Onny Meadows, which are
well worth an exploratory detour. Here, pick
up a laid path on the right-hand side of the
meadows for 400m, parallel with the A49
away through the trees on the right, to a
path junction. A right turn takes you across
the A49, up a lane, past the Church of St
John the Baptist, which is well worth a visit,
and round the bend to Stokesay Castle. This
timbered and yellow-panelled house is one
of the oldest and finest examples of a
fortified manor house in the Marches, and
you'll often have seen its façade on posters

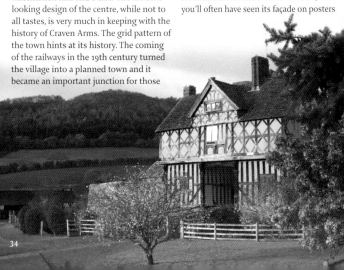

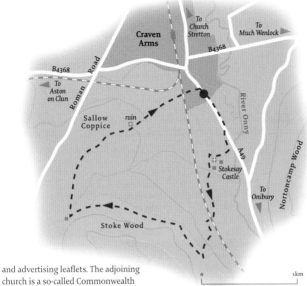

and advertising leaflets. The adjoining church is a so-called Commonwealth Church – it was rebuilt after Cromwell's men had finished with it, though somehow the house escaped largely unscathed. If visiting the castle, it would be feasible to start the walk from here, though it is worth noting that the castle's car park is gated when the castle is closed.

The onward route continues along the lane past Stokesay Castle to an unmanned crossing over the mainline railway after 500m. Beyond, a byway climbs uphill towards Stoke Wood. Here, turn right through a barrier onto a broad track for a 1.5km section that initially contours the edge of the woodland, with good views over Stokesay and the Onny Valley, before rising gently to a house at the western

limit of the wood at Clapping Wicket.

A footpath off to the right now takes you over a series of fields – head diagonally across the first two fields with Caer Caradoc Hill and Hope Bowdler Hill on the horizon; in the third field turn right along the fence and descend for 600m along a shallow dry valley over fields to the ruin of a red-brick house, Paddock. From here you'll need to veer a little to the left and over the rise to hit the stile into the final field. At the far end by a spreading oak tree a track leads off right, passing under the railway and into a small housing estate, before bringing you back to the road opposite the Discovery Centre.

◄ Stokesay Castle

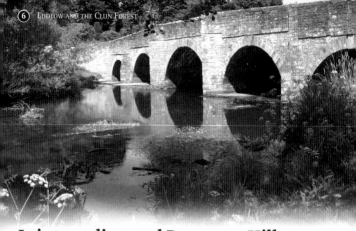

Leintwardine and Downton Hill

Distance 6.5km **Time** 1 hour 45
Terrain lanes, tracks and woodland
Map OS Explorer 203 **Access** bus (498, 802)
from Hereford and (738, 740) from Ludlow
or Knighton

The village of Leintwardine lies across a
medieval stone bridge, just downstream
from the confluence of the Rivers Teme
and Clun. Close to the border with Wales
and surrounded by fortified hills, there is
a real sense of place and history here.

The old road, which runs parallel to the
main A4113 up through the village, is still
called Watling Street. Indeed, it has long
been known that the current village lies on
top of the Roman site of Bravonium, as
recorded in the *Antonine Itinerary*, a Roman
road atlas. The OS map for the area prints
the alternative name, Branogenium, and
this is the name assigned to the place by
the geographer Ptolemy. Whichever name

was actually used, you can still see hard
evidence of Roman occupation in the
Norman doorway of the west wall of the
Church of St Mary Magdalene. Here, you'll
find the tell-tale thin Roman bricks,
reclaimed from some building or ruin and
placed either side of the window. Of
interest inside the church, which you pass
at the end of the walk, are carvings on the
roof timbers and pillars in the nave, some
decorative stone screens flanking the east
window, a disused 16th-century clock, and
in the vestry a memorial to Sir Banastre
Tarleton. To some he has come to be
known as 'Bloody Ban', following his
reputation for military ruthlessness in the
American War of Independence, though
some recent books and films have treated
him in a more heroic light.

From the bridge over the River Teme
walk along Rosemary Lane for 550m, past
the bottom of Watling Street and The Sun,

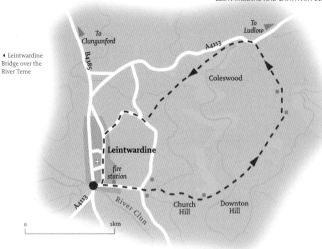

◀ Leintwardine
Bridge over the
River Teme

an old parlour pub, and then the fire
station, to the bend and junction at the
foot of Church Hill. Here, a footpath leads
up the right-hand edge of a field, before
zigzagging its way up alongside the
woodland and past a very small quarry to a
gate at the top, with good views south over
the Teme Valley. The route, climbing more
gently now, follows the field edges before a
fenced and hedged section brings you past
a barn and house on the left.

From here, for the next 2.25km, a track
takes you northeastwards along the right-
hand edge of the broad ridge above the
settlements of Downton, with views to the
Clee Hills and down to Ludlow. The track
veers to the left at a prominent bend by a
house, before continuing up over a
crossroads and the rise beyond, from
where it descends, passing Mocktree Barns
to reach the A4113.

Turn left down the road for 50m, where a
track leads off to the left. Look out for a
bridleway on the right of the track which
heads down through the trees of
Coleswood. The bridleway joins a wider
track after 300m and carries on down to the
edge of the woodland, where a gate leads
into fields. Follow the wooded left-hand
edge of the first field, with the tower of
Leintwardine Church visible ahead, then
keep to the left into a second field with its
substantial hedge to your right. At the far
end, ignore the track off left and keep
straight on along the bridleway for another
250m to a narrow lane. Here, a right turn
leads past houses, round the left-hand bend
and on to a junction with Dark Lane and
Watling Street. Now turn left back down
Watling Street, from which you can detour
off right to see the church.

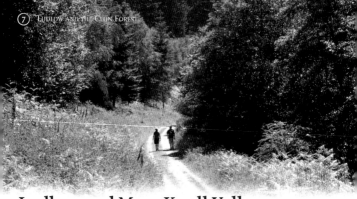

Ludlow and Mary Knoll Valley

Distance 9km Time 2 hours 30 Terrain woodland, tracks and fields Map OS Explorer 203 Access train from Hereford or Shrewsbury, bus (492) from Hereford, (435) from Shrewsbury or (740) from Knighton

Take in this most celebrated of border towns before escaping to the tranquility of the surrounding fields and woods.

As a town, Ludlow contains a near embarrassment of history. The most obvious features are the Norman castle, for centuries the seat of the Lords President of the Marches and a major link in the long line of castles from Chepstow to Chester, and the celebrated Church of St Laurence known locally as the Cathedral of the Marches. In front of the church, the Buttercross stands at the head of Broad Street, one of the finest Georgian townscapes in the country. From here, the medieval narrow streets give way to Castle Square, which still hosts a weekly market, with the town's museum located on its southern side.

From Castle Square, walk down Dinham Road, following the castle walls past Dinham House and the 12th-century Chapel of St Thomas to the bridge over the River Teme. Here, to the right over the Millennium Green, is the site of the former Dinham Mill and a café, where you can still see the working waterwheel. Across the bridge, bear left for Whitcliffe Common onto the Mortimer Trail. At the top of the steps, fork right along the edge of the common for 250m to the road. Here, turn right to the junction at the bend, then left up Lower Wood Road for just 50m, where the Mortimer Trail branches left up through the forest for the next 800m (at the first fork after 30m, keep right), before heading up to the left, across the road and up the access track to Mortimer Forest Whitcliffe car park.

At the bend, bear left to stay on the Mortimer Trail and the gently rising main track heading southwestwards. After 500m, leave the trail and branch right along the signed grassy track of the

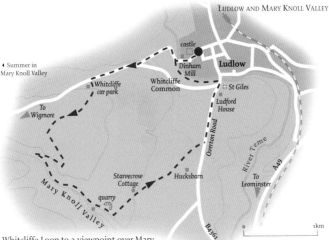

◄ Summer in
Mary Knoll Valley

Whitcliffe Loop to a viewpoint over Mary Knoll Valley. Go left downhill for 200m to rejoin the main Mortimer Trail. This heads southeastwards to a crosspaths after 75m, where a path veers right and drops to a junction with the bridleway at the bottom of Mary Knoll Valley.

Turn left onto the bridleway which, for 1km, twists gently down the steep-sided wooded valley beside a stream and past a large pool to a track junction with a cottage on the right. Here, bear left uphill past an old quarry and, at the hairpin bend beyond, take the hedged bridleway to the right. You soon start descending and pass the pretty cottage of Starvecrow, where the bridleway runs along and between fields for another 500m to a track junction. A left turn takes you past the entrance to Hucksbarn and along the top of a field, with good views over Ludlow to Clee Hill. Near the end of the field, take the path on the left through the gate into woodland and down past a

house to Overton Road (B4361).

Now turn left along the pavement for 800m towards the southern edge of Ludlow. Just past the gates and chimneys of Ludford House, you can detour right to the church of St Giles, worth seeing for the impressive Charlton tombs.

At this point you can either go over the bridge and up Broad Street or, to return to Dinham Mill, turn left at Ludford Corner, where it is easy to miss the small plaque commemorating Sir Roderick Murchison, the pioneering 19th-century geologist who used the so-called 'Ludlow Rocks' in his great seven-year work on the geological timescale of the Silurian period. Continue for just 20m and, on the right, climb some steps back into Whitcliffe Common, then bear right down to the 'Breadwalk' riverside path back to Dinham Bridge.

Titterstone Clee Hill

Distance 8km **Time** 2 hours 30
Terrain moorland paths, tracks and quarry
edges **Map** OS Explorer 203 **Access** bus
(292) from Ludlow or Kidderminster

**Step back into the past on a moorland
walk, with the marks and scars of human
history littering the landscape.**

The walk starts from the viewpoint and
car park on the A4117 on the eastern edge
of Cleehill village. Perched high on the
hillside, the village grew up around the
quarrying of coal, ironstone and
dhustone. The name means 'black stone',
from the Welsh *dhu*; the hard dolerite rock,
ideal for road-building, is capped in places
by coal-bearing layers. Titterstone Clee Hill
itself, being the second highest hill in the
area at 533m, is a perfect site for the radar
station which controls the region's air
traffic. The hill has been used throughout
history as a vantage point – you can still
see the remnants of Bronze and Iron Age
monuments and structures – and it is the

only named hill on the 14th-century *Mappa
Mundi*, displayed in Hereford Cathedral.

From the car park, a path leads east for
75m to the viewpoint before heading up
across the A4117 past the Craven Place
tearooms onto a bridleway beside a private
road. Once around the large flooded
quarry, the track emerges onto open moor.
At this point leave the bridleway, which
bends right, and follow a path NNE – in
clear weather, you can see the landmark
Three-Forked Pole on the skyline, marking
the boundary of the parishes of Bitterley,
Caynham and Coreley. Initially, the wide
path leads up over the base of an old slag
heap, becoming less distinct as it climbs
the moorland slope towards the pole.

From here, the onward moorland route
is pathless for 1km. With the radar station
on the skyline as your guide, head
northwestwards over the broad grassy top
of Clee Hill and then bear slightly right for
300m into a dip, aiming for the prominent
angle in the fence by marshy Willmore

◀ Old slag heaps near the head of Titterstone Incline

Pool. The going is slightly awkward, but once at the fence a quad-bike track leads onto the access road and up to the radar station on Titterstone Clee Hill.

To the left of the radar station a path squeezes along the fence (avoid a loose path further left up the quarry side itself) and skirts the rim of the large quarry, whose sides are steep and eroded. Bear left around the cliff edge to pick up the tarmac access road past the remaining radar installations and above a second quarry. Here, the Shropshire Way comes in from the left and heads up to the triangulation point on top of Titterstone Clee Hill, with the Giant's Chair a little further on to the right and a view to Brown Clee Hill. Both these points stand on top of Bronze Age burial cairns and, looking about the plateau, it is easy to see the remnants of other mounds and hollows. Indeed, encircling the upper section of the hill are the remains of a man-made bank of dhustone along with at least 15 other burial cairns.

The onward route runs back along the Shropshire Way and down the ridge between the two quarries to a hairpin bend in the access road – you can detour to the right to explore the old mining complex above Titterstone Incline. To continue, walk down onto the moorland road for 1.75km as it curves round the head of the

valley and descends southwestwards along Dhustone Lane past the houses of Rouse Boughton Terrace.

At the bend beyond the houses, look out for a bridleway off left. This leads up onto the track of the former Dhustone Incline railway and contours past quarry workings and the backs of houses for 1.2km to the south of Clee Hill. At the lane by Railway Cottage, with the Kremlin Inn up to the left, turn right to return to the A4117 and Cleehill village.

41

The Welsh border presses eastwards here, making Knighton and Presteigne true border towns, with the Teme Valley initially marking the northern boundary of this section, before it loops northwards back into Shropshire. In the west the former county of Radnorshire marks the start of hill country, while the River Lugg, flowing eastwards from Presteigne, takes you through the heart of Mortimer Forest, the former powerbase of the Marcher Lords of the Mortimer family. The countryside of northwestern Herefordshire around Wigmore and Richards Castle is now often cited as quintessentially English in its blend of hills, valleys and farmland, though its history from Norman to Tudor times tells a more brutal story of conflict and struggles for power. Further south the area is full of small villages and secluded settlements whose origins stretch back to the Saxons, Romans and the Celts.

Old cider press and mill, Shobdon ▶

Knighton, Presteigne and Mortimer Forest

1 Knighton and Garth Hill   44
A small but perfectly-formed stroll
from this walker-friendly town

2 Norton and Hawthorn Hill   46
Pack a picnic and stride out on this
higher-level route

3 Wigmore   48
There's plenty to see on this short
up-and-down route and it's ideal for
the kids too

4 Richards Castle   50
Walk in the steps of medieval
townspeople and through some of
Herefordshire's prettiest countryside

5 Croft Ambrey Fort
and the Fishpool Valley   52
A popular route that's just perfect for
a short stroll

6 Presteigne and Harley's Hill   54
A hands-in-pockets walk above this
Marches market town

7 Shobdon Arches Loop   56
A great little stroll with an
architectural surprise or two en route

8 Titley   58
Starting from a quiet village, green
lanes and fields quickly take you away
from it all

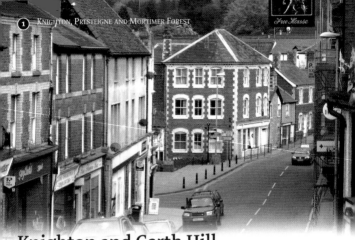

Knighton and Garth Hill

Distance 5km **Time** 1 hour 30
Terrain lanes and paths through woods
and fields **Map** OS Explorer 201
Access train to Knighton from Cardiff or
Shrewsbury, bus (738, 740) from Ludlow
or (41) from Kington

**A short walk of contrasts from a true
border town, with its train station across
the River Teme in England and its castle
in Wales.**

Long-distance walkers are spoilt for
choice in Knighton. Offa's Dyke Path
passes through on its north-south
journey across Wales, while Glyndwr's
Way winds a circuitous route for 217km
northwestwards towards Machynlleth,
where Owain Glyndwr himself was hailed
as leader of Wales in 1404, before
travelling eastwards to Welshpool. If you
want to find out more, the Offa's Dyke
Centre on West Street is a good place to

start, and it has a car park to the rear.

The first part of this walk follows the
initial section of Glyndwr's Way. From the
clocktower in the centre of Knighton, walk
up the steep pedestrianised High Street,
along which there is an informative notice
board about the trail.

At the top, the route turns left into
Market Street before descending Castle
Street, past the site of the town's old
motte and bailey castle, to a narrow
walkway at the bottom which bears right
between the stream and some pretty
cottages. It's a simple task to follow the
waymarks for the next 500m as the route
soon veers right up through the housing
on the town's southern edge, over the
B4355, and then up a fairly steep path to
emerge onto a lane at a bend.

Here, a quick dogleg right, then left
keeps you on Glyndwr's Way as you now
bear north above the town. The path soon

◀ Knighton town centre

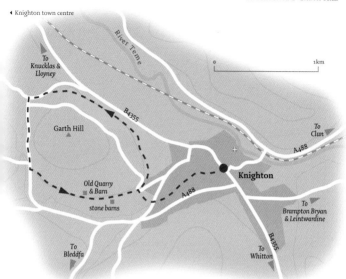

enters some pleasant woodland and contours around the north side of Garth Hill. Through gaps in the trees, there are views across the Teme Valley to Panpunton Hill and the line that Offa's Dyke takes as it aims for the Clun Forest. After 1km you leave the woods behind and start to rise gently to reach a lane.

Bear left up to the junction and then left again, still on the route of Glyndwr's Way. With the very top of Garth Hill up to the left, this hands-in-pockets lane drops down between hedges and fields for 600m into a steep-sided wooded dell. Where a lane merges from the right you now leave the route of Glyndwr's Way and take the footpath on the left.

This path, which can be muddy at times, follows a fence along the hill's southern side between the higher open ground and the enclosed fields below. After 600m you pass a barn in an old quarry on the left and cross over the top of a track leading down to Brookhouse Farm, before crossing the next field to some attractive old stone barns. Just beyond, pick up a track which climbs up over the short rise and, at the top, bear right over a stile and down to the lane. Here, to return to the start you can turn right back onto Glyndwr's Way and the outward route or, to avoid the climb back up Castle Street, walk down the lane ahead and back along the town's streets.

45

Norton and Hawthorn Hill

Distance 8km Time 2 hours 30
Terrain lanes, tracks and fields
Map OS Explorer 201 Access bus (41) from
Kington and Knighton

Save this walk for a clear day and leave
plenty of time for taking in the views as
you follow a well-preserved section of
Offa's Dyke.

The walk starts opposite the church in
the village of Norton, 7km north of
Presteigne, where there is a small lay-by on
the B4355. The church is worth a visit,
though its Victorian rebuilding in the
Gothic style by Richard Green-Price, 1st
Baronet and philanthropist of nearby
Norton Manor, and the architect George
Gilbert Scott, of St Pancras Station and
Albert Memorial fame, was controversial at
the time and still divides opinion. One of

the south windows has a memorial to the
1st Baronet and the churchyard contains
the family graves, perhaps proving the
motto on the sundial on the south wall of
the tower – *Disce Bene Vivere et Mori* (Learn
how to live and die well).

Walk along Mynd Road which, after
200m, becomes a track and bridleway and
heads uphill, passing a left fork down to
Norton Manor, now a hotel. Continue
along the main track for another 500m to
Old Impton Farm, where the bridleway
passes to the right of the farmhouse.
Beyond, bear to the right up a field to a
track, before continuing on the bridleway
steadily uphill in a WNW direction along a
fence and into Impton Wood.

At the top of the wood, turn right up the
field to a gate in the fence at the top, where
a fingerpost marks the route of Offa's Dyke

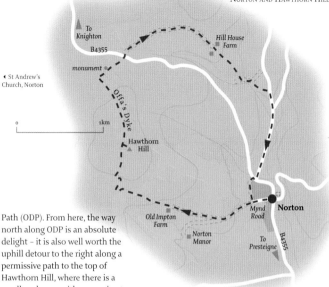

To Knighton

B4355

Hill House Farm

monument

◀ St Andrew's Church, Norton

Offa's Dyke

0   1km

Hawthorn Hill

Old Impton Farm

Norton Manor

Mynd Road   **Norton**

To Presteigne

B4355

Path (ODP). From here, the way north along ODP is an absolute delight – it is also well worth the uphill detour to the right along a permissive path to the top of Hawthorn Hill, where there is a small enclosure with some pine trees, a picnic table and one of the best views in the Marches. On a clear day it is possible to see as far as the Brecon Beacons and the Cotswolds.

Offa's Dyke Path itself follows a line northwards just below the hill's broad ridge, soon passing to the left of a small plantation and along a surviving section of the dyke itself, before veering a little northwest and descending gently for 700m to pass between two small patches of forestry. Here, you should leave ODP and bear right, heading northeast, onto a bridleway where, 100m ahead, a granite monument to Richard Green-Price serves as a convenient marker. From here continue for 200m to a lane.

The onward route bears left and crosses the B4355, where the bridleway leads to Hill House Farm. Pass between the farm buildings and, just before the last sheds, turn right down two fields to cross a stream onto a track. Here, dogleg left on the track for 50m and then right across two more fields to reach a lane. A right turn, downhill for 1km, leads to a junction with the B4355 just north of Norton.

From here, the left turn along the verge of the road back into Norton is perhaps best avoided. Instead, cross the road and dogleg right, then left up Maes Offa cul-de-sac. At the bend, keep ahead along a walkway to its junction with Mynd Road and then turn left back to the start.

Wigmore

Distance 5km Time 1 hour 30
Terrain lanes, fields and woodland tracks
Maps OS Explorer 203 and 201 Access bus
(491, 802) from Leintwardine and Hereford

Explore the past of this historic medieval
village before circling over fields and
through woods.

The walk starts from the centre of
Wigmore village, 6km south of
Leintwardine, where there is parking at
the village hall along Ford Street.
Following the signs for the church and
castle, walk up Church Street and through
the churchyard. The medieval church of St
James is well worth a look inside for the
herringbone masonry in the north wall of
the nave, the linenfold panelling on the
16th-century pulpit and the unusual
arrangement of pews in the chancel.

Beyond the church, continue up the
lane past some cottages and take the
signed path to Wigmore Castle for 200m
to a pair of kissing gates, where you can
detour right, up some steps and through
the gateway to the ruins of the castle
beyond. It is now under the management
of English Heritage who have recently
made considerable efforts to preserve
what remains of the gatehouse, the walls
and the towers. By design, it has been left
in a somewhat wild condition and this is
all to the good for those who like to think
of castles as places of bygone romance
and intrigue. The place was home to the
powerful Mortimer family, the so-called
Lords of the Marches, who added
significantly to the buildings during the

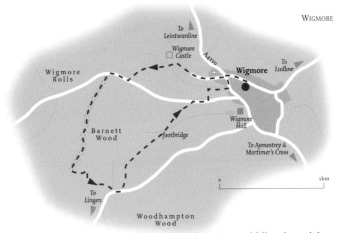

12th to the 15th centuries. However, it was deliberately destroyed in the 17th century during the period of the Civil War to prevent it being used as a base by Royalists. For those wanting more in the way of history, rather than romance, dotted around the site are a number of English Heritage information boards.

The onward route follows a fenced track to the left of the castle to a field. Here, head up the slope, bearing a little to the right, past some trees to a stile. Cross a second field, passing under some electricity wires, up to a stile and gate onto a lane. Now dogleg right along the lane for 100m to a bend, then left along a track into the deciduous Barnett Wood. Pass through a barrier and follow the main track for 600m as it twists steadily uphill, ignoring paths off to the side. At the top of the rise, bear to the right and follow the track gently down for another 250m until you reach a dense conifer plantation. Now turn sharp left downhill,

steeply at times, and follow the track for 500m all the way to the lane on the southeastern edge of the wood.

The route now bears left along the lane for just 20m and then accompanies a well-signed footpath on the left into fields to the east of the wood. Following the waymarks, make for the top of the first field and along the right edge of the second, before heading diagonally left down a large third field and over a stile into a small dell, where there is a footbridge over a little stream. Across the water, head diagonally right, in a northeasterly direction, up the slope of this large fourth field to a stile in the hedge onto a lane.

From here, dogleg right down the lane for 100m, then take a footpath on the left into fields again. After 50m the path zigzags right, then left to drop downhill between hedges to a track and stream at the bottom. Here, a right turn takes you past Brook Farm and back into Wigmore.

◀ The former gateway to Wigmore Castle

Richards Castle

Distance 8km Time 2 hours 15
Terrain lanes, tracks and fields
Map OS Explorer 203 Access bus (492)
from Ludlow and Leominster

This quiet corner of Herefordshire contains many surprises in its undulating folds, not least a lost medieval town.

The hamlet of Richards Castle lies between Ludlow and Leominster on the B4361, where there is some parking in a lay-by 300m up past the Castle Inn on the lane which leads to the church and castle.

The walk, initially following the route of the Herefordshire Trail, carries on up the lane for 900m, passing the entrance to Court House Farm, over a crossroads and more steeply uphill towards Green Farm, named after the triangular piece of ground here which was known from medieval times as The Green and marked the centre of the old village. Just past the farm buildings, bear left up a short track to Old Church Cottage. From here, you can take a

detour ahead through a gate up to the church and castle.

It is hard to imagine that there was ever a substantial medieval town here but, after flourishing for 300 years, decline set in as the nearby towns of Ludlow and Leominster dominated the area in trade and political importance. The church of St Bartholomew is now well-known for its detached belltower. Abandoned at the end of the 19th century it has nevertheless been well-preserved and it is worth having a look inside at the 17th-century box pews. For those wanting a detailed tour, the Churches Conservation Trust have produced an excellent explanatory leaflet, available at the rear of the church. There is also an informative Millennium Map on the southern edge of the churchyard, with interesting snippets about the area's history and associations. The remains of the castle, one of the oldest in Wales and already in ruins by the 16th century, lie just a little further on beyond the graveyard.

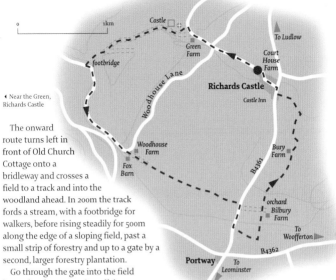

0   1km

Castle

Green
Farm

To Ludlow

Court
House
Farm

footbridge

Woodhouse Lane

Richards Castle

Castle Inn

◄ Near the Green,
Richards Castle

Woodhouse
Farm

Fox
Barn

Bury
Farm

B4361

orchard
Bilbury
Farm

To
Woofferton

B4362

Portway   To
Leominster

The onward route turns left in front of Old Church Cottage onto a bridleway and crosses a field to a track and into the woodland ahead. In 200m the track fords a stream, with a footbridge for walkers, before rising steadily for 500m along the edge of a sloping field, past a small strip of forestry and up to a gate by a second, larger forestry plantation.

Go through the gate into the field beyond and, now turning off the Herefordshire Trail, bear left over the rise and steeply down to the bottom of the field, where a footbridge leads onto a lane. Turn left down the lane for 1.25km, passing through bluebell woods lower down and keeping left at a crossroads, to the bend with Woodhouse Farm beyond.

Here, a bridleway bears half-right off the lane (ignore the footpath sharp right up the field), down past Fox Barn, through the houses beyond and onto a track on the far side of the farm buildings. The bridleway now heads over three fields in an ESE direction for 1.3km, initially as a track and then as a path along the field edges. The route then goes straight across the middle of the fourth field, passing over the rise ahead and down to the B4361.

Turn right for 200m along the road, where, round the bend, a path leads left across a field to a junction with the Herefordshire Trail. Turn left and again follow this waymarked trail as it heads northwards to Bilbury Farm, across its driveway and over three more fields to pick up a track leading to Bury Farm. Pass to the right of the farmhouse and, 100m beyond, dogleg left, then right along the right-hand edge of the next field. Cut left across the far end of this field and up through a small orchard to reach the B4361 again. Here, a dogleg right and then left up the lane past the Castle Inn leads back to the start.

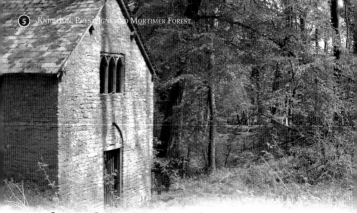

Croft Ambrey Fort and the Fishpool Valley

Distance 4km Time 1 hour 15
Terrain woodland and parkland
Map OS Explorer 203 Access no bus service

A stroll through a landscaped wooded valley leads to a commanding Iron Age hillfort, with the lure of the Croft tearoom to guide you back to the start.

This walk starts from the National Trust car park at Croft Castle, for which there is a charge, near the village of Yarpole. The Croft Estate has belonged to the Croft family for 30 generations and contains the ancient Croft Ambrey Fort. Its occupation dates back 2500 years and the slopes are studded with old beech, oak and chestnut trees. The Fishpool Valley leading to the hillfort is particularly scenic and in the late 18th century it was landscaped to include ornamental structures such as a grotto and pump house, having in medieval times contained a series of fish pools. Croft Castle itself is a 17th century castellated manor house, though there was an actual castle, or series of castles, built on the site from Norman times, whose earthwork remains can be seen in the meadow nearby. It is easy to combine the walk with a visit to the house itself, with its Gothic interior and the period furniture, paintings and country-house paraphernalia you would expect. There is also a tearoom and children's play area.

Setting out from the bottom end of the car park, go back through the roadside gate by the cattle grid and bear left down the hill for 200m on a woodland path to a junction with a track in the Fishpool Valley. The route now heads left onto the waymarked Mortimer Trail, up the track on the left of a stream and past a series of pools, reaching some former limekilns after 450m. Ignore the left fork here, instead keeping right to pass the kilns and

◀ In the Fishpool Valley

a brick pumphouse before coming to a junction after 400m.

At this point bear left, still following the Mortimer Trail, up a wooded dell for 600m, crossing two forestry tracks to a gate at the top of the slope. Turn left along a permissive path for just 50m before crossing a stile on the left, now leaving the Mortimer Trail. From here, a path takes you up to the top of Croft Ambrey Fort with its impressive earthworks and views. The defences are still a sight, even after more than two millennia. Excavations have brought to light the usual artifacts of an Iron Age hillfort, tools, weapons and pottery. However, archaeologists have also

uncovered many post holes, indicating there may have been several hundred people living on the site at any one time.

To continue, descend the southwestern slope of the earthworks, bearing slightly left down to a stile and a track beyond. Turn left for 150m along the track to a fork junction and bear half-left over a stile into Park Wood, which is managed by the Forestry Commission. The route heads SSE through the wood for 500m, passing over a rise and down over a crosspaths to a kissing gate by some old pollarded chestnut trees at the wood's southern edge. Go through the gate and take the permissive path ahead that descends the left edge of the field for 300m, passing more old chestnut trees at the bottom. Here, pick up a track that travels down through the parkland towards Croft Castle and its car park and tearoom.

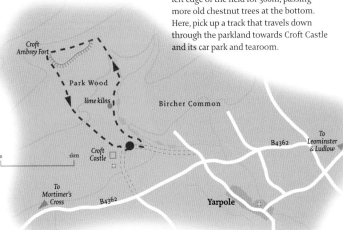

Flowers by Cynthia   St Micha

Presteigne and Harley's Hill

Distance 5km **Time** 1 hour 30
Terrain lanes, woodland and fields
Map OS Explorer 201 **Access** bus (493)
from Leominster and (463) from Kington

A bit of puff is required for the climb from this scenic border town, but the hard work is soon over and it's downhill on the way back.

The route starts in the centre of Presteigne by the clocktower at the junction of Broad Street and the High Street. Presteigne itself is a delightful border town on the River Lugg, with a smattering of cafés and local antique and craft shops for diversion if the weather is against you.

The walk heads off along the High Street past the Radnorshire Arms Hotel. Local lore has it that a certain John

Bradshaw, one of the regicides and indeed president in 1649 at the trial of Charles I, once had lodgings here. Buried in Westminster Abbey, at the Restoration he was disinterred and given a posthumous hanging by the followers of Charles II for his stiff republicanism. Keep on round the left bend up to the main road that bypasses the town. Cross over and head up Warden Road, where you can turn right to explore The Warden. A path runs over the mound of this former motte and bailey castle. It was destroyed in the 13th century in a campaign by Llewelyn ap Gruffydd, who had proclaimed himself prince of Wales in 1258. However, when Edward I acceded to the English throne in 1277, Llewelyn's territory was invaded and he was eventually killed seven years later after a failed rebellion. Now a town park

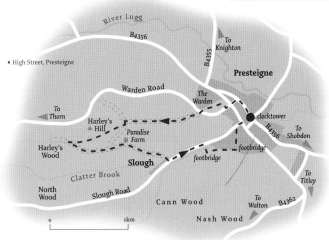

River Lugg

B4356

To
Knighton

Presteigne

◀ High Street, Presteigne

Warden Road

The
Warden

clocktower

To
Thorn

Harley's
Hill

Paradise
Farm

To
Shobdon

Harley's
Wood

footbridge

Slough

footbridge

Clatter Brook

North
Wood

Slough Road

Cann Wood

To
Titley

To
Walton

B4362

Nash Wood

0   1km

covers the slopes with its trees, picnic tables, and bluebells in the spring. Head down the far side to rejoin Warden Road, 300m further along at the mound's western entrance.

From this entrance continue up Warden Road for another 50m before turning left uphill along a lane that carries a bridleway. The lane soon becomes a hollow-way (if this is very muddy use the field path that runs parallel on the right for 400m) and continues to climb for 650m, through a gate and up to a fork in the path near the northern tip of Harley's Wood. Bear left at this fork and then in 30m, at a second fork, keep right to follow the path along the wood's northern edge. In 400m, just after passing a fenceline coming down from the right and the triangulation pillar marking the top of

Harley's Hill, look out for a marker post.

Here, bear left down through the trees to a junction with a bridleway, where a left turn downhill takes you to a fork in the path just before Paradise Farm. Bear right off the bridleway and head to the far end of the farm, where its driveway leads downhill to the right and in 600m reaches the quiet lane of Slough Road.

Turn left along the lane for a little over 500m and, just before a housing estate, turn right along the edge of a field for 75m and across the Clatter Brook. Now turn left onto a pleasant path along the brook's right bank. After 300m the path crosses to the other bank. Here, bear left along a track that leads back to Slough Road, where a right turn soon takes you to an underpass that leads back to the centre of Presteigne and the start.

55

Shobdon Arches Loop

Distance 6km Time 1 hour 30
Terrain lanes, fields Maps OS Explorer 201
and 203 Access bus (493, 496) from
Leominster, Presteigne and Kington

A Norman folly and some gaudy 'gothick'
architecture provide a striking diversion
on this short circuit from Shobdon.

The walk starts from the village of
Shobdon, which lies on the B4362 mid-
way between Leominster and Presteigne.
There is a car park at the western end of
the village behind the village stores and
post office.

Head along the road through the village
to its eastern end, past the Methodist
Church to the timber-framed Bateman
Arms. Across the road, a gated driveway
and waymarked circular route leads up
through parkland and some ornamental

ponds to the buildings of Shobdon Court
and Shobdon Church. The interior of the
church, with its decoration in the style
known as Strawberry Hill Gothick, comes
as a complete surprise, one that is
perhaps liked or loathed. There is a
guidebook available for those wanting
detailed explanations of the architecture
and the history.

The onward route continues ahead
up a grassy tree-lined avenue to the
famous Shobdon Arches, with an
incongruous food factory away to the left,
which may leave you wondering how it
ever received planning permission in such
a scenic spot. These are the remains of a
Norman church and they were moved
here in the 18th century to form a
Romanesque folly with a picturesque
viewpoint. Now faded, but still visible,

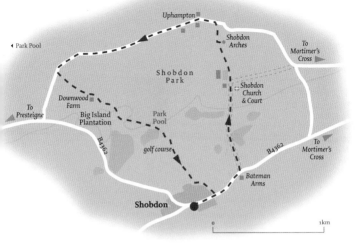

you can see the 12th-century carvings on the semi-circular tympana and the supporting pillars.

A little to the left of the Arches a path carries on through woodland for 100m to a lane. Turn left along the lane through the hamlet of Uphampton to some large farm sheds. Here ignore the circular route waymarked off right up a track and continue along the lane for another 1.2km, with views right to Shobdon Hill and Wood.

At a prominent left bend with a track leading off right to Belgate Farm, take the footpath branching left over fields. At this point the circular waymarked route is rejoined. Head in a southeasterly direction over fields, following the waymarks, to pass above the buildings of Downwood Farm. Here,

ignore a path returning east to Shobdon Church, but continue down over more fields, with the buildings of Downwood away to the right, and then bear left to pass along the northern edge of the Big Island Plantation. Go along the right-hand edge of the next field for 250m, past Park Pool which is half hidden in the trees on the right, and look out for a stile in the fenceline on the right which gives access to the golf course.

Across the stile, a dogleg left, then right takes you up the edge of the fairway – watch out for wayward golf balls here – and along a line of trees to the top of the golf course. Here, turn left along the edge of two small fields before heading to the right to reach a stile and path which leads between houses to School Lane and back to the centre of Shobdon.

Titley

**Distance 5km Time 1 hour 30
Terrain fields and lanes, with one steep
climb Map OS Explorer 201 Access bus
(41) from Kington or Knighton**

**Stride out on this easy walk from a quiet
village, tucked away between the valleys
of the Arrow and the Lugg.**

This well-signed circular walk initially
follows part of the Mortimer Way and
starts by the church at the northern end
of the village of Titley, where there is a
lay-by for parking.

Take the footpath that leads past the
end of the church and up the hill ahead
along field edges. The fairly stiff gradient
means you quickly gain height, but it
soon eases off as the path heads across
fields over the brow of the hill and down

towards the buildings of Green Lane
Farm and a junction of lanes. The view
from the top on a clear day allows you to
look south back over the Arrow Valley,
while to the northeast lies Wapley Hill,
whose slopes holds an Iron Age fort.
Indeed, it is possible that occupation of
the site of Green Lane Farm itself dates
back to this period and may have been
part of a long line of forts and farms in
the Marches, all linked by a network of
walking and trade routes.

Here, the route doglegs left, then right
to continue westwards along Green Lane.
Initially broad, this lane soon becomes a
pleasant tree-lined way between fields
and there is a feeling that this route has
seen the passage of
people, horses and

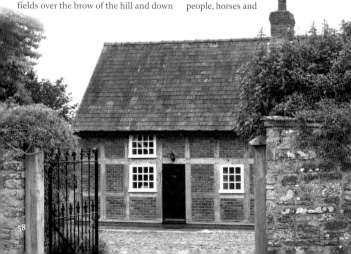

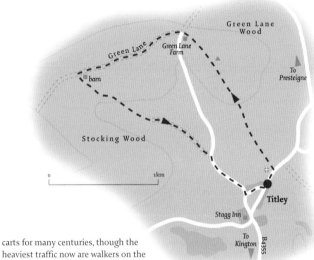

Green Lane
Wood

Green Lane

Green Lane
Farm

To
Presteigne

barn

Stocking Wood

0   1km

✝

Titley

Stagg Inn

To
Kington

B4355

carts for many centuries, though the
heaviest traffic now are walkers on the
Mortimer Trail and farm vehicles, which
can make it rather muddy when wet. After
passing a small pool on the left, the track
rises to the magnificent stone barn of
Burnt House.

Just beyond the barn, a fingerpost signs
the way left to Titley. Head down through
a small copse to emerge at the top of a
series of fields that extend down the floor
of a dry valley, whose vista is laid out
ahead. The path is clearly signed here,
though after the first field you have to
peel away from the top edge and descend
diagonally right, before crossing three

more fields to pick up a grassy track. In
winter the field edges may be a less
muddy alternative. The track proves easier
going and leads past an old quarry,
emerging after 600m onto a lane.

Here, turn right downhill for 500m
and then left along School Lane to return
to the church, or continue straight on
to the southern end of the village, if
The Stagg Inn beckons – in 2001 it was
the first English pub to be awarded a
Michelin star.

◀ In the village of Titley

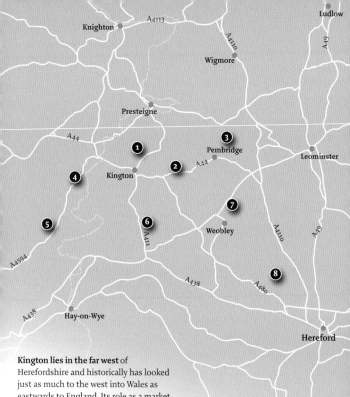

Kington lies in the far west of Herefordshire and historically has looked just as much to the west into Wales as eastwards to England. Its role as a market town is somewhat diminished, though with Offa's Dyke Path passing close by it now promotes itself as a centre for walkers and ramblers. The moorland slopes that rise to the town's west are the outliers of the chain of hills stretching through central Wales and provide some longer and more challenging routes, while eastwards to the River Lugg and southwards to the Wye Valley lie many of the so-called black

and white villages for which Herefordshire is well known, especially Pembridge, Eardisley and Weobley. The countryside here is gentler and amongst the arable crops you'll still find plenty of cider-apple orchards and small cider producers for which the county is so famous.

Wain Wen Farm above Gladestry ▶

Kington and West Herefordshire

1 Hergest Ridge and Castle Twts   62
A bit of puff is needed at the start, but the rewards are worth it on this classic airy round

2 Lyonshall and Offa's Dyke   64
Perfect for a short walk or to stretch one's legs after a leisurely lunch

3 River Arrow meander   66
A mostly level route between two of Herefordshire's most interesting villages – Pembridge and Eardisland

4 Gladestry and Colva Hill   68
You'll probably only have moorland birds for company on this higher-level route from the village of Gladestry

5 Newchurch Hills   70
A stout pair of legs is needed for this undulating route around the Arrow Valley

6 Eardisley loop   72
Take in some of Herefordshire's most scenic countryside and villages

7 Burton Hill   74
Stride out on this longer route from Weobley – one of the country's best-preserved Tudor towns

8 Credenhill Park Wood and Fort   76
A short walk suitable for any season and an ideal one for the kids

Hergest Ridge and Castle Twts

Distance 11km **Time** 3 hours
Terrain lanes, grassy slopes, field and
woodland paths **Map** OS Explorer 201
Access bus (41) from Knighton, (495)
from Leominster, (461) from Hereford
and New Radnor

**Pick a clear day for this classic and hilly
round above the town of Kington for one
of the best viewpoints of the English-
Welsh border.**

The market town of Kington is situated
in the Arrow Valley in the far west of
Herefordshire. Enclosed to the north by
the hills of the Radnor Forest and to the
west by the high ground of Hergest Ridge
(pronounced Hargist), the town has long
been part of England even though it lies
to the west of Offa's Dyke, with the
modern Welsh border only a couple of
miles away.

Legend has it that the name Kington, or
King's Town, commemorates the
confiscation of lands by Harold
Godwinson (later of Battle of Hastings
fame) who made a gift of the area to King
Edward the Confessor after a Welsh attack
on Hereford in 1055, in which the city was
sacked by the forces of Llewelyn of Powys.
The town itself grew up between the River
Arrow, flowing to the south of the town,
and the Bach Brook to the north, and lies
on the old drovers' route from Wales to
the English markets of Herefordshire.
Indeed, Kington's cattle market used to
take place on Bridge Street and the former
commons of Hergest Ridge made the
town a favoured stopping point.

From the Market Hall with its
clocktower in the centre of Kington, head
up Church Street past St Mary's Church
and turn left up Ridgebourne Road, where
there is a fingerpost for Offa's Dyke Path,
which leads to the top of Hergest Ridge.

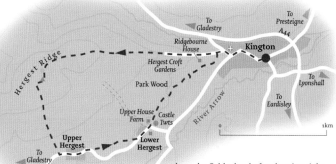

A steady pace is required as it is a long pull up past Hergest Croft Gardens to a gate, beyond which a grassy path leads up the open slopes for 2km to the hill's northeast top, marked by a crosspaths, a commemorative bench and some puzzling trees. The higher top lies 800m to the southwest – in the dip ahead bear left by a small pond – and has a triangulation pillar, though the very highest point lies 200m to its west. Needless to say, in mist this can be a confusing place.

The onward route descends a bridleway on the hill's southern slopes. From the marker near the highest point, head down through the gorse and grass, looking out for another marker post in 200m, where the route becomes better defined, veering left to a gate and a track down to a lane.

Here, a left turn leads in 600m past the buildings of Upper Hergest (ignore a bike route down to the right) to a sharp right-hand bend. Now take the waymarked route straight on along a track and then along the field edge, before bearing right across the top of a second field and then diagonally down to reach the lane again. A left turn leads through Lower Hergest to a junction and bend. Ahead, through the gate, lies the prominent mound of Castle Twts. Its top gives a good vantage point and time to puzzle at the unusually diminutive stature of this Norman motte and bailey.

The route descends on a footpath to the left of the mound and then, clearly waymarked, climbs up along field edges and diagonally down to the edge of Park Wood. Here, a track descends to an ornamental pond and up again before descending to the left of Park Wood Cottage to a cattle grid. Now zigzag along the track, right, then left for 50m, before turning right onto a footpath which heads over the parkland of Hergest Croft House. The right of way veers a little to the left along the boundary wall of Ridgebourne House, across its former driveway and then back to Ridgebourne Road, where a right turn takes you back onto the outward route.

◀ St Mary's Church, Kington from the grounds of Hergest Croft

Lyonshall and Offa's Dyke

Distance 4.5km Time 1 hour
Terrain lanes, orchards and fields
Map OS Explorer 201 Access bus (461) from
Kington and Hereford, (495) from Kington
and Leominster

Perfect for stretching the legs, this short
stroll takes in one of the best-preserved
sections of Offa's Dyke.

The village of Lyonshall is situated on
the main A44 between Kington and
Pembridge. Its church and 11th-century
castle stand with a cluster of houses and
farm buildings alongside the main A44
road itself and it was here that the
medieval village stood. However, the
modern village has grown up a little down

the lane to the south and is somewhat
incongruously separated from what was
originally its centre.

From the Royal George Inn, walk
southwestwards along the lane out of
Lyonshall towards Eardisley and
Bollingham for 500m, passing an old
chapel. At a cottage, a footpath on the right
leads through a gateway onto a track
beside a stream and an orchard. After
200m, as the track bends left, the path
carries straight on up the side of another
orchard and, just short of the far end, bears
right across the top of the neighbouring
field and up to a lane. Cross the lane and
continue up the left edge of the
field ahead alongside

a prominent section of Offa's Dyke. Even today, it is easy to gauge the scale of this still sizeable rampart. King Offa's 8th-century dyke stretched from the estuary of the River Dee in North Wales all the way south to the mouth of the River Wye and, combined with rivers and natural high ground, formed a visible and striking frontier for his kingdom of Mercia. At this point, the earthwork crosses the lower-lying land of Herefordshire, though even here it often runs against the grain of the country and its construction would have been a considerable undertaking.

Where the dyke peters out look out for a marker post. Here, dogleg left, then right through a gate and along the field edge, before bearing right along the edge of a second field to reach the busy A44.

On the opposite side of the road, take the path between Lyonshall Nurseries and a red-brick house to reach a gate. The route now bears right over several small fields and in 400m reaches the Church of St

Michael and All Angels. To the northeast of the church stand the remains of Lyonshall Castle. There is no public access to the site, though a good view of the ruins can be had from the northern edge of the churchyard.

To continue, walk down to the A44 and, on the opposite side, take the lane to the right of a black and white timbered house. After 150m, look out for a path which leads left, down across a field and then slightly left through an orchard. Cross the next field to pick up a track which passes for 100m between some houses and emerges onto the lane opposite the old chapel passed on the outward route. A left turn brings you back into the centre of Lyonshall.

◄ Church of St Michael and All Angels, Lyonshall

65

River Arrow meander

Distance 8km Time 2 hours
Terrain field paths and lanes Maps OS
Explorer 201 and 202 Access bus (493, 495,
496) from Kington and Leominster

Riverside meadows and lanes combine to
make this the most enticing of routes
between two black and white
Herefordshire villages.

The village of Pembridge is very much
on Herefordshire's Black and White
Village Trail and is well-known for its old
timbered buildings, not least the Market
Hall in the small square behind the New
Inn. It is not so much a hall as a covered
meeting area and, following recent
dendro-dating analysis, it was estimated
to have been built in the first third of the
14th century, making it possibly the
oldest market hall still to be in regular
use in the country. In the posts you can
see notches where planks for traders used
to be placed. Goods would have been
displayed on these and, at the

foot of one of the posts, there is also what
is thought to be one of the original mark
stones, from which the word 'market'
stems. In addition, the earthen floor is
unusual in its survival. There is plenty
else of interest in the village, including
the church and its detached belltower,
whose octagonal lower staging and
wooden boarding come as something of a
surprise and are perhaps more
reminiscent of Scandinavian stave
churches than anything local.

Start from the Amenity Trust car park
just behind The King's House pub on East
Street in Pembridge. A gate at the rear
leads past a children's play area, alongside
houses and down across two fields to a
gate onto Long Meadow beside the River
Arrow. Here, the route takes you to the
right over the broad open fields for the
next 1.75km. The waymarked
path initially crosses the
middle of the fields, with the
river away to the left, before

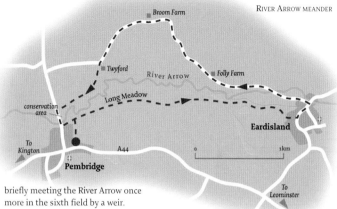

Twyford River Arrow Folly Farm

Long Meadow

conservation
area

Eardisland

To
Kington A44

Pembridge

0 1km

To
Leominster

briefly meeting the River Arrow once more in the sixth field by a weir.

From here, continue along the field edge with a small stream on the left for 150m before bearing right with the path to the start of a small copse. A dogleg right, then left over a double stile takes you along the edges of two more fields, where a left turn into a third field leads to the houses and road running through the village of Eardisland. A left turn along the pavement leads past The White Swan pub and The Cross Inn to the bridge over the River Arrow. The community has recently overseen the restoration of the Georgian Dovecote which stands near the bridge, and this serves as an information and exhibition centre. As in Pembridge, there are a good number of timber-framed buildings – Staick House across the bridge dates from the 14th century, Bridge Cottage used to be the grammar school and the Old Manor House has a somewhat incongruous Queen Anne frontage. To continue the walk, turn left just before the bridge down Broom Lane

alongside the pretty riverside houses. This soon becomes a narrow and twisting country lane which makes for delightful hands-in-pockets walking for the next 3km. Initially it crosses and then shadows the River Arrow before veering north and then turning west, just before the buildings of Broom Farm, and then southwestwards to a sharp right-hand bend at Twyford. Here, leave the lane and go down the house's driveway for 50m, where a waymarked path branches right over three fields to a lane. Here, a left turn takes you to the bridge over the River Arrow.

If time and interest allow, it's worth pausing here to wander the boardwalks of Pembridge's small hay meadow and wet woodland conservation area. To return to the start, you can either brave the traffic and head up Bridge Street to the village centre and East Street or turn left for 150m along the river's south bank to reach Long Meadow once again, from where you can retrace the outward route.

Gladestry and Colva Hill

Distance 10km **Time** 3 hours 30
Terrain country lanes and moorland
tracks **Maps** OS Explorer 201 and 200
Access bus (42) from Kington (limited
service)

**If you're after solitude, stride off into
these bracken- and heather-covered
moorland hills, but pack a map and
compass in case the mist comes down.**

The walk starts from the village of
Gladestry, which lies at the foot of
Hergest Ridge on the B4594 about 10km
southwest of the town of Kington. There
is parking available at the roadside lay-by
near the school or near the village hall
opposite the church. In the centre of the
village is the Royal Oak Inn and the Old
Post Office, which is now a small and
friendly shop serving snacks and teas. In
the summer it's open fairly regularly; at
other times just ring the bell and see if
the owners are in.

From the centre of the village, walk up
past the Church of St Mary and take the
first lane on the left, which heads round
the back of the church. In 300m, as the
lane starts to climb gently, keep right
where the lane forks. From here it's a
pleasant stroll along the hedged lane for
the next 1.5km, past the entrance to Wood
Farm, to a second fork. Here, bear left up
an even narrower lane, which in 200m
branches right and becomes a track
climbing above Pen-faen Brook to a gate
onto the open hillside, which marks the
start of a Site of Special Scientific Interest.

From here don't be tempted to continue
up the broad bracken-covered ridge but
instead bear to the left, initially along a
fence, where a path makes a rising
traverse for 800m up to the head of
Cwminon and a track junction on the
eastern edge of an area of bog called the
Mawn Pools. From this point you are on
high, open moorland, where it would be

◀ The high moorland of Colva Hill

easy to become disorientated in poor visibility and confident navigation may require the use of a map and compass.

From the pools take the track heading WNW for 200m around the right-hand side of the bog to the point where a path heads off left along the line of some metal boundary posts, which lead you WSW for the next 600m. Where the posts make a sharp left turn, keep ahead for another 50m to a crosspaths. Here, turn left (ESE) and climb the slope ahead to the track's high point and some extensive views – a triangulation pillar marking the very top of the hill lies 50m to the right.

To continue, follow the narrowing track for 700m down to a T-junction with a vehicle track. Here, turn right and head southwards and then southeastwards for 1.5km on this broad track, which initially contours the hillside but soon starts to descend on the left-hand side of a steep valley before circling down round the prominent lump of Carreg Gwyn to a gate. Pass through the gate and down the rough field's fence for another 250m to the point where a track, the old road from the settlement of Colva, comes up from the right.

Head left for another 250m up over the grassy moorland, where the track is really just a muddy line, to a gap in some stands of woodland. From here a clear continuation of the track winds its way down to Wain Wen Farm and then joins the twisting lane beyond for 1.5km, across the dip of Pen-faen Brook and back to Gladestry.

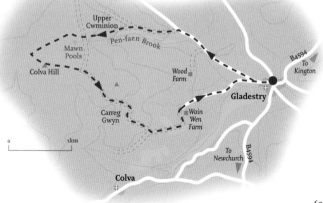

Newchurch Hills

Distance 9km Time 3 hours
Terrain lanes and tracks, with two hill
ascents Map OS Explorer 201
Access no bus service

You'll soon leave any 'Offa's Dykers'
behind as you peel off the well-beaten
track on this high round of the hills above
the Arrow Valley.

The walk starts from the small village of
Newchurch, situated to the north of Hay-
on-Wye on the B4594 between Painscastle
and Gladestry. The village has become a
draw for walkers and visitors, not only
because Offa's Dyke Path passes through
but also because of the reference in Francis
Kilvert's 19th-century diary to the tragic
death of Emmeline Vaughan and the yew
tree which he thought stood weeping over
the grave. The yew tree was toppled in a
storm 20 years ago, but a plaque in the
church still commemorates the story.

From the church in the centre of the
village walk down the road and pick up
signs for Offa's Dyke Path (ODP) heading
northwards. Round the bend, bear right
onto a track up past some farm buildings
to a gate onto the open hillside. It's a bit of
a pull up to the southern top of Disgwylfa
Hill, but then the grassy path down across a
dip and past an often dried-out pool makes
for easy walking to the main top and a
panoramic view, with Hergest Ridge visible
to the north and the Arrow Valley cutting
through the landscape to the south.

To continue, follow the route of ODP for
another 400m down the far side of the hill,
but, where the national route turns left,

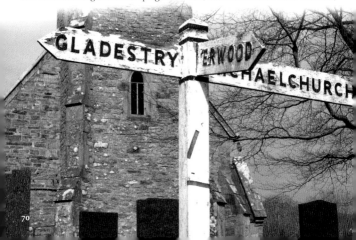

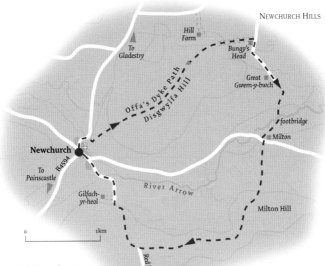

Newchurch

carry straight on down to a stream and gate onto a track, which in 400m leads to a junction with a lane at Bungy's Head.

A right turn down this pleasant lane leads you over a cattle grid and then a stream, before reaching the impressive farmhouse at Great Gwern-y-bwch, beyond which the lane becomes a track and leads to a field-gate. Here, bear right and then descend diagonally over the fields to a footbridge over the River Arrow.

Once across the river, a right turn over more fields now takes you up towards the hamlet of Milton. At the lane, dogleg left past Milton House to the bend and then right onto a bridleway, which marks the start of the second climb of the walk. The route up Milton Hill is initially a delightful hollow-way up to a gate on the edge of the open hillside. Here, keep right at a fork in

the path, heading straight up the bracken-covered slope, over a boggy patch of ground and up to a marker post on the top of Milton Hill. The route now crosses the dip ahead to reach the main ridgeline, where a right turn along a track makes for gentler walking, though this section can be muddy in wet conditions.

After 1.5km along the ridge, you reach a path junction where ODP joins from the left. This well-marked route now points the way back to Newchurch and soon tracks northwards over fields, with extensive views in clear conditions, before descending towards the farmhouse at Gilfach-yr-heol and the top of an almost permanently muddy track. At the end of the track a narrow lane twists its way for 750m back down to Newchurch.

◀ In the village of Newchurch

Eardisley loop

**Distance 9.5km Time 2 hours 30
Terrain fields and lanes
Map OS Explorer 201 Access bus (462)
from Hereford or Kington**

**An undulating walk through fields,
farms and ancient woodland between
two of Herefordshire's prettiest villages.**

Eardisley is well known for its black and
white timbered buildings, including the
Tram Inn at the northern end of the
village which is named after the 19th-
century Brecon to Kington horse-drawn
tramway. In addition, the New Strand Café
and Bookshop is something of a draw and
there is also an old pumphouse and some
cruck cottages at this end of the village.

However, at the southern end stands the
Church of St Mary Magdalene and this
contains an extraordinary example of
Herefordshire Romanesque carving on its
early 12th-century font. The main scene
depicts the Harrowing of Hell – Christ,
holding a cross with a dove on his
shoulder, is pulling the hand of a small

figure, identified as Adam, with the
additional figures of a lion, representing
evil, and God the Father holding a book.
A second scene shows a pair of armed men
fighting and is thought to be a possible
reference to a duel between two local
families, the Baskervilles and the Cliffords.

From the centre of the village opposite
Bridge House, take the path which squeezes
its way between some houses and a stream,
before crossing a field to a tree-lined
embankment. A left turn along the line of a
former tramway takes you northwards and
across Almeley Road. Now follow the
curving field edge for 300m until a marker
post directs you left to a second field, where
a line of trees shows you the way. Near the
top of the field you'll need to branch right,
down to a footbridge over the stream in
Holywell Dingle.

The woodland path climbs the far side a
little way before bearing left and then rising
and falling as it makes its way upstream for
700m to a bridge and information board.
At any time of year, this ancient coppice

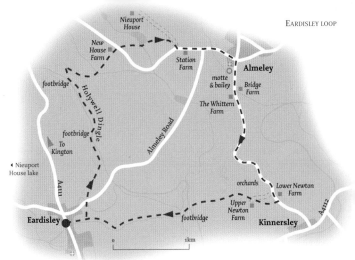

woodland, with its mix of deciduous species, makes for pleasant walking, but it is perhaps at its best in spring with its covering of wildflowers. From the bridge, the route takes the path that climbs right, to the top edge of the wood and on for 50m to a stile.

You now head diagonally right across a field to a track in the far corner which, after 450m, cuts through the buildings of New House Farm, across the road and over two more fields into woodland again. Amongst the trees the private ornamental lake of Nieuport House comes as something of a surprise, but it makes a good point for a rest before taking the path at the far end which bears off to the right – avoid the track ahead. Go through a gate and head diagonally across more fields, with views ahead to the village of Almeley, down to a house and lane. Here, a left turn past Station Farm takes you

over a crossroads, past the buttresses of a railway bridge and then Batch Cottage, previously home to tramroad and railway workers, and on into Almeley, where you'll find a pub, The Bells Inn, the site of an old castle and a fine church.

At the junction by the church, turn right down the twisting lane for the next 2km between fields and orchards and up to the hamlet of Newton. At the far end of Lower Newton Farm look out for a path on the right into fields and follow the waymarks diagonally right, through an orchard and across the drive of Upper Newton Farm to a stile to the left of a red-brick house.

The route now heads diagonally across the first field and up through another orchard, before descending three fields to a footbridge over a stream on the left. From here, follow the well-signed path over another series of fields back to the embankment on the edge of Eardisley.

Burton Hill

**Distance 12.5km Time 3 hours 15
Terrain fields, lanes and woodland, with
one hill Map OS Explorer 202 Access bus
(461, 462) from Hereford and Kington**

**A longer outing up steep slopes from one
of the finest villages in Herefordshire to
the prominent skyline of Burton Hill.**

The village of Weobley is on every map
showing Herefordshire's black and white
villages and it is perhaps one of the best
surviving examples of a Tudor town in
the country. For parking, head for Bell
Square, just off the B4230 at the
northwestern end of the village, where
there is an information board and
opposite you'll see the Manor House, one
of the oldest buildings in Weobley. The
centre is dominated by Broad Street,
which used to be narrower but the houses
that occupied the middle strip burned
down and have been replaced by a
pleasant garden. At the street's lower end
is the Church of Saints Peter and Paul.
Famous for having the second tallest spire
in Herefordshire, it is just as noteworthy

for its pinnacles which are connected to
the tower by flying buttresses, with an
appearance similar, if of smaller scale, to
Hereford Cathedral itself.

Start from the top of Broad Street,
where a path to the left of Ye Olde
Salutation Inn leads through the mounds
and dips of the town's old motte and
bailey castle. From here, with views of
Burton Hill ahead, discs for a local circular
walk initially mark the way southwards
for 1km over the fields of Garnstone Park,
a former deer park, to woodland.

Bear right to follow a track for 100m to a
house, where you should go sharp left,
diagonally up the field behind to a gate in
the top corner. Just beyond here, the route
leaves the local circular walk and turns
right up a track which, after a stile, curves
right as it climbs to a gate into woodland.
Follow the clear track as it winds its way
around the north side of the hill for the
next 1km – after 500m ignore a marked
path off left and, in another 200m, at a
fork with a marker post, keep left uphill.
As the path levels out, swing round to the

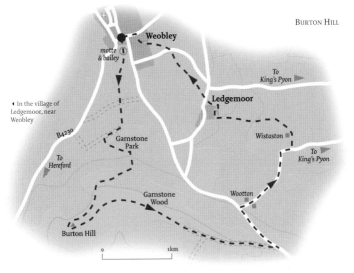

Weobley

motte & bailey

To King's Pyon

Ledgemoor

◀ In the village of Ledgemoor, near Weobley

B4230

Wistaston

Garnstone Park

To Hereford

To King's Pyon

Wootton

Garnstone Wood

Burton Hill

0   1km

left for the triangulation point marking the top of Burton Hill.

For the next 1.5km, a grassy permissive path continues through the mixed woodland along the broad crest of the hill and over a crosspaths, before bending right and climbing gently to the wood's eastern edge. Here, a left-hand field edge takes you past an old barn to a track, with good views to the Black Mountains and down the valley towards Hereford, and then onto a lane which leads down to a road junction in 1km.

Turn left down the hill for 800m and then right along a pleasant lane (SP King's Pyon) which leads past the farm at Wootton, with views to Westhope Hill. Then 150m after a sharp right bend, take the lane branching left up to Wistaston. At the rear of the buildings a path leads diagonally across a field and then turns

left, initially along the field edge, but after 200m you'll need to cross the fence and then a small stream to continue across two more fields to reach a lane in the hamlet of Ledgemoor.

Here, turn right up the lane to a house at the end, where the path has to circle to the right between gardens and then twice left to reach the field behind the house. Head diagonally left across this field with a view to the spire of St Peter and Paul's Church. Across the next lane, the local circular walk is rejoined as you take the right-hand path over three fields and along the fenceline of two more, before crossing a third lane and two more fields. Now bear right along the back of the housing estate, where the path soon becomes a tarmac walkway up to the road. A left turn leads back past the Unicorn Inn to the centre of Weobley.

Credenhill Park Wood and Fort

Distance 3km Time 1 hour
Terrain woodland tracks and paths
Map OS Explorer 202 Access bus (71, 461, 462) from Hereford to Credenhill Village (750m from start of walk)

Step back in time for a glimpse of how life was lived 2000 years ago when Celts and Romans clashed.

Credenhill Park Wood is a steep wooded knoll topped by an Iron Age hillfort, situated to the northwest of Hereford. Access to the Woodland Trust car park at its southeastern corner is easiest from Credenhill Village, where a narrow lane (SP Tillington) leads off the A480 – the car park and picnic area are 400m along on the left.

Credenhill is now mostly covered with trees, though this is more the result of the decline of the practice of coppicing and the policies of woodland management in the 20th century, when the majority of the broadleaved trees were felled and large numbers of conifers planted. Now the Woodland Trust is starting to restore the area to native trees. The hillfort itself is one of the largest in Britain, enclosing about 70 acres, and its location suggests that 2500 years ago it may have been the tribal capital of the Decangi tribe. Recent tree clearance has revealed hidden earthworks, in addition to the obvious rampart and ditch which encircle the hill, and archaeologists have estimated that several thousand people could have inhabited the place when the Romans suppressed the tribe in the middle of the 1st century AD and established the Roman town of Magnis (modern Kenchester), which lies just 2km to the south.

The path begins at the rear of the car

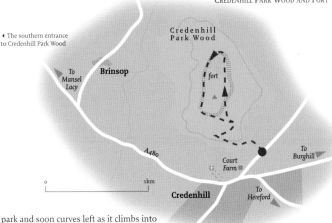

◀ The southern entrance to Credenhill Park Wood

park and soon curves left as it climbs into the woodland. After 400m, at the second track junction, curve sharp right with the main track as it continues to climb, past a marker post indicating no route for horses and up to a stock gate across the track. Beyond the gate you soon pass through the outer earthwork rampart of the hillfort. Keep on the main track as it curves to the right and continues to climb before levelling out, with the hill's high point away to the left in the trees.

A little further on you come to the edge of a cleared area, with some modern wooden stockades. The Woodland Trust has introduced Highland Cattle, along with sheep, not in an attempt to recreate an authentic sense of Iron Age living conditions, but rather as a practical measure to restrict the regrowth of trees, whose roots were beginning to damage sections of the hillfort. The hope is that a grassland area can be established as the animals eat saplings. The result for

walkers, apart perhaps from any surprise on seeing the beasts, is the opening up of some fine views, especially westwards to the hills of Mid Wales and the Black Mountains and northeastwards to the ridge of the Malvern Hills.

Continue across the cleared area of rough grassland to the obvious rampart on the far side and bear left down to some steps up onto the rampart itself. The route now heads left along the top of the rampart on the western edge of the clearing and into the woodland once again. From here it's a simple task of following the rampart, though there are three gaps to cross, each with a set of steps to negotiate. After the third gap the rampart curves to the left and in 250m brings you back to the main track, where a right turn downhill through the stock gate passed on the way up allows you to retrace your steps to the start.

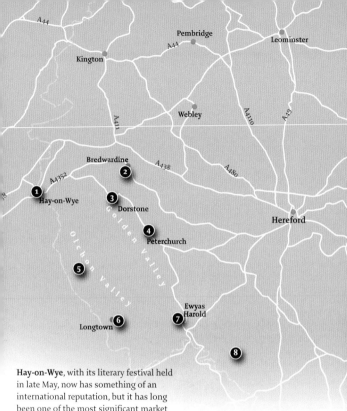

Hay-on-Wye, with its literary festival held in late May, now has something of an international reputation, but it has long been one of the most significant market towns of the Marches. Not only does Hay-on-Wye lie right on the border between England and Wales, it also sits on the northern edge of the Black Mountains, which now form the eastern section of the Brecon Beacons National Park and provide some of the most accessible hillwalking in southern Britain. These are true hills and the northern ridges give stunning views on clear days, while hidden away in the folds of the land from the Black Mountains northwards to the River Wye you'll find the secluded Upper Monnow and Golden Valleys. Far less visited than other parts, this area is criss-crossed by narrow lanes and dotted with small villages, many with farms, churches and castles dating from Norman times.

Arthur's Stone burial chamber, above Bredwardine and Dorstone ▶

Hay-on-Wye and the Golden Valley

1 **Hay-on-Wye and the Warren**   80
If you need an antidote to bookshops, try this riverside stroll

2 **Merbach Hill and Arthur's Stone**   82
The climb may be long, but the views go on and on too – save this one for a clear day

3 **Vagar Hill**   84
You'll most likely have the views all to yourself from these high fields and open moorland

4 **Peterchurch and Blakemere Hill**   86
Wander through woods and fields high above the Golden Valley

5 **Black Hill and the Olchon Valley**   88
A short walk that has it all – an airy ridge, fine views and a hidden valley

6 **Longtown and the Mynydd Merddin**   90
Explore the Monnow Valley and the less-frequented high pastures on the edge of the Black Mountains

7 **Ewyas Harold Common**   92
Historic village and ancient common combine to make this a stroll to take your time over

8 **Garway Hill and Jack O'Kent**   94
Walk in the footsteps of a folklore giant and see seven counties from one of the best viewpoints in the southern Marches

Hay-on-Wye and the Warren

Distance 3.5km **Time** 1 hour
Terrain town lanes and riverside paths
Map OS Explorer OL13 **Access** bus (39)
from Hereford and Brecon

When you've had your fill of the bookshops and cafes, try this short riverside meander – it's also perfect for children and there's even a beach.

The town of Hay-on-Wye lies right on the English-Welsh border, and literally so, as now the centre and the western parts of the town lie in Wales, while some houses in the eastern part are in England. In fact, the town used to be known as English Hay and the countryside to the west of the town as Welsh Hay, with the Welsh name for the town being Y-Gelli, which means

'grove'. For centuries it was a market town surrounded by its walls and dominated by the Norman castle, whose walls and keep, albeit subsequently significantly altered, still tower over Castle Street. However, it is now best known for its plethora of bookshops. New, secondhand and antiquarian shops litter the town and you can find just about any volume you would wish in the 30 or so that now operate here – even the castle and the old cinema have been converted.

From the main car park by the tourist information centre, turn right along Oxford Road by the side of Hay Castle's northern wall and down past the Bethesda Church to the eastern edge of town. At the bend, the route doglegs left along Lion

◄ In the former grounds of Hay Castle

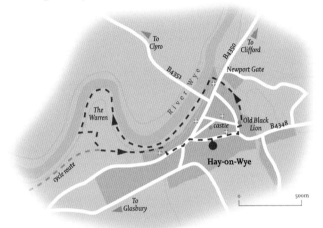

Street and then right down beside the Old Black Lion pub. At the fork in this narrow lane, bear left and follow the path along the line of the town's medieval walls. A few remnants are still visible just before the B4350 and the former Newport Gate.

The route crosses the road and heads down Wyeford Road to the river, where a left turn takes you under the roadbridge and along a pleasant tree-lined path above the Wye. At the gate into the Warren keep right. The path soon comes down to the water's edge and leaves the trees behind, before skirting around the wide open space of the meander. It's a delightful spot for a picnic, and people come here to paddle and swim, when river conditions allow.

Near the apex of the meander, it's best to take the upper path over the headland and away from the water's edge. At a stile cross over and bear left for 100m on a path that shadows the fence and stone wall to a vehicle track. Here, a right turn will soon bring you to the buttresses of a bridge of the disused railway, which is now a cycle route.

Turn left along the disused railway and after 500m look out for a small waterfall on the right, where a path to its left takes you up past the grassy mound of Hay's old motte and bailey castle. From here, a left turn leads back to the town centre.

Merbach Hill and Arthur's Stone

Distance 8km **Time** 2 hours 30
Terrain steep start; lanes and field paths, with two steeper sections of descent
Map OS Explorer OL13
Access bus (447, 448) from Hereford

A long ascent from the Wye Valley leads to a ridgetop amble with far-reaching views and an equally steep descent.

East of Hay-on-Wye and lying to the south of the A438 in the Wye Valley on the B4352 is the easily-bypassed village of Bredwardine. A beautiful 18th-century bridge spans the River Wye, notable as one of the oldest brick-built bridges still standing. Walkers pass through here on the Wye Valley Walk, while visitors to St Andrew's Church often come in search of the grave of the vicar and diarist Francis Kilvert. There is also an old motte and bailey castle just beyond the church and, a little way up from both the river and the church, a 17th-century brick-built former coaching inn, The Red Lion, stands on the once busy crossroads.

The first section of the route up to the top of Merbach Hill follows the Wye Valley Walk, waymarked with a leaping salmon symbol. From the lane to the church, where there is space for parking, walk up over the crossroads with the B4352 past the Red Lion Hotel. The lane's 1 in 4 gradient soon gets your heart pumping, though at a bend after 600m a right turn onto a bridleway brings a gentle descent to a gate at another bend. Here, the climb resumes as you head left beside a stream over fields to a track into woodland.

This pleasant track takes you up past Woolla Farm, where it bears left and

◀ Springtime in the village of Bredwardine

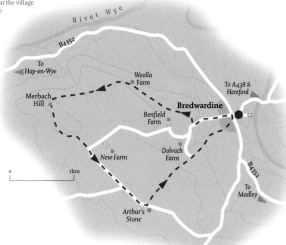

steepens once again up to a junction. Here, keep ahead past a corrugated barn and over three fields to the start of the open common. A short dogleg keeps you on the twisting path. After 500m, look out for a low marker post at a triple fork – the central path (leaving the Wye Valley Walk) leads up to the triangulation pillar of Merbach Hill, from where there are superb views north over the Wye Valley.

The route now bears left (south) onto the route of the Herefordshire Trail and more level walking. Head through the jumble of small pits to a gate into a large field, whose right-hand edge should be followed for 800m as it bends left to a lane. Here, keep straight ahead and enjoy the views and easy walking for 1.1km to the obvious bend, beyond which lie the

remains of a Neolithic burial chamber, known as Arthur's Stone. Thought to be more than 4000 years old, its siting is as impressive as its antiquity and on a clear day the views from the high ground extend over the Black Mountains and deep into Monmouthshire.

To continue, take the field edge footpath opposite and then bear northeastwards down six more fields (in the fifth, descend steeply alongside some woodland) to a house. Carry on down the lane and pass to the right of the farm buildings, before swinging back left across a small stream and descending another steep field to its bottom left corner, where the route veers right to a timber-framed house and track to Bredwardine.

83

Vagar Hill

Distance 11km **Time** 3 hours 30
Terrain fields, moorland tracks and lanes
Map OS Explorer OL13 **Access** bus (39)
from Hereford and Brecon

Take your binoculars for some wildlife spotting on Vagar Common as well as for making the most of the impressive panoramic views.

Commanding the head of the Golden Valley is the village of Dorstone. There is a triangular village green with a market cross, topped by a sundial, the old school is now the village hall and behind this is an old motte and bailey castle to explore. The pub, the Pandy Inn, is still thriving and has been since the 12th century when Sir Richard de Brito built an inn here during his construction of the village church as part of his penance for the murder of Archbishop Thomas a Beckett in Canterbury Cathedral in 1170, making it perhaps the oldest pub in the county. The current church is the third on the site and dedicated to St Faith – likely to have been identified with the Celtic Saint Moy, which to Norman ears was similar to Foi, and hence 'Faith'. The church also used to have a rare 13th-century coffin chalice, though this was stolen in 2005 and only an old picture of it remains.

A path to the right of the village hall leads past the impressive mound of the village's tree-topped motte and bailey castle and continues over two fields towards farm buildings. Dogleg right, then left through the farm and up into delightful Mill Wood by a small stream. Some 150m beyond a gate, the route bears left with the fence up to Penlan Farm.

Here, waymarkers take you to the left of the farm buildings and up over four more fields to reach a lane. Turn right and then left at the bend to follow this lane over a crossroads and all the way to the top of Vagar Hill, with its triangulation pillar,

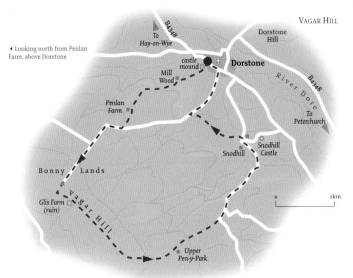

◄ Looking north from Penlan Farm, above Dorstone

communications masts and fine views.

To continue, walk 150m further along the track and through a gate before turning left along a rough track that follows the broad crest of Vagar Common for 1.5km, with long views down the Monnow Valley. The ruins of Glis Farm and the scarp of the Black Mountains beyond are perhaps a reminder of the isolation of hill-farming here, though now horses as well as sheep are grazed on this high moorland. This grazing is essential to help maintain the acid grassland habitat, which supports such wildflowers as heath bedstraw, tormentil and sheep's sorrel. However, bracken is increasingly taking over and has to be cut back, not only for the flora but also for groundnesting birds such as skylarks, snipe and curlew. In addition, around here,

you may well see buzzards and red kites circling overhead.

At the southeastern end of the ridge, just beyond a small pond, bear left with the fenceline downhill for 1.8km, soon switching to fields on the left and passing near to the ruined cruck-frames of Upper Pen-y-park, to a stile onto a lane. The lane leads steeply down to the ford in the village of Snodhill, where it bends left up to a crossroads. Here, you can detour right for 400m to visit the remains of Snodhill Castle.

From the crossroads, the route now bears left in 30m onto a bridleway and the waymarked Herefordshire Trail, along a track and over fields and two streams before turning right down Pitt Road. At the junction, a left turn leads back to the centre of Dorstone.

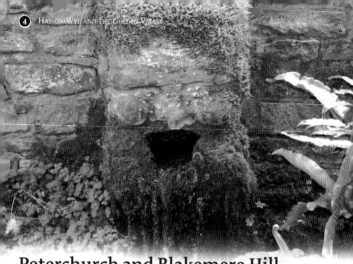

Peterchurch and Blakemere Hill

Distance 6.5km Time 1 hour 45
Terrain lanes, woodland tracks and fields
Map OS Explorer OL13 Access bus (39)
from Hereford and Brecon via Hay-on-Wye

A steady ascent soon gets you up to the fields and woodland high above the Golden Valley before a descent past a sacred well.

The village of Peterchurch is set in the heart of the Golden Valley and the spire of its church is a landmark for miles around. The river along the valley is the Dore, an unusual name, possibly from the French, though the etymology is more likely to be from the Welsh *dwr*, meaning 'water', or from *ystrad-our*, meaning 'place of gold'. However, there may be a wholly natural and visual explanation for the name – try travelling through the valley on a late

summer's evening when the fields are full of wheat about to be harvested.

The walk starts from the car park on Church Road next to a picnic area and children's playground. Head up Church Road to the B4348 and turn left along it for 600m, past the Boughton Arms to the Nag's Head pub at the western end of the village. Here, the route turns right along Mowbage Lane and soon becomes a pleasant track that climbs uphill to reach Greenway Farm after 800m. Ignoring the footpath ahead, bear right with the track up past some modern farm buildings. The track now levels off and doglegs left and then right, before heading down to a gate at the western edge of Rough Leath Wood.

Go through the gate and take the bridleway that forks left past Rough Leath Barn before circling round to the right and

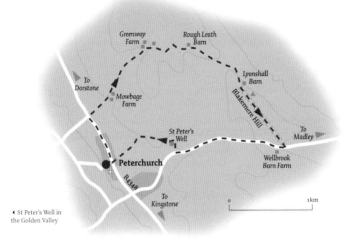

Greenway
Farm

Rough Leath
Barn

To
Dorstone

Mowbage
Farm

Lyonshall
Barn

Blakemere Hill

St Peter's
Well

To
Madley

Peterchurch

B4348

Wellbrook
Barn Farm

To
Kingstone

0   1km

◀ St Peter's Well in
the Golden Valley

bearing southeastwards down through the plantation on a path that can be muddy. Cross a forestry track and continue for 400m along the bridleway (or the track running parallel to it, which it anyway joins after 300m) and up to a gate at the wood's southern edge. Beyond, pass the revamped Lyonshall Barn and walk up to the triangulation pillar on the left of the track. This makes a good spot to pause and admire the great view over the Golden Valley to the Black Mountains.

The onward route follows the straight track ahead, which descends gently for 700m to a lane and has good views eastwards to the Malvern Hills. At the lane, turn right past the entrance to Wellbrook Barn Farm, over the brow of the hill and down the other side to the point after 1.4km where a track joins from the right

just before a left bend. Bear right along the track for a short way before crossing a stile into the neighbouring field on the left to continue up to St Peter's Well. This was once something of a sacred spot and sufferers from rheumatism used to come here to bathe, though you have to use your imagination somewhat to picture this now.

From the well, carry on to the top of the field and rejoin the track on the right, just short of a junction in front of the house ahead. Here, bear left along a grassy track between fields. This soon becomes a hollow-way and descends gently past a cottage on the right to a track junction 30m beyond, where a left turn downhill takes you, with the spire of St Peter's ahead, past Bazley Farm and back to the centre of Peterchurch opposite the Boughton Arms.

Black Hill and the Olchon Valley

**Distance 8km Time 2 hours 30
Terrain steep ascent and descent,
moorland paths Map OS Explorer OL13
Access no bus service**

**An airy ridge walk on the northern edge of
the Black Mountains with fine views,
open moorland and a hidden valley – it
makes an ideal round for youngsters.**

The Welsh name for this most northerly
of the ridges of the Black Mountains is
Crib-y-Garth. It means crest of the ridge
and aptly describes the airy walk to be had
along its sandstone outcrops. However, the
hill has also come to be known locally as
the Cat's Back. The reason often given for
this unusual name is that, when viewed
from the north or the south, the outline of
the hill forms the shape of a cat arching on
its haunches. Sceptics of such

etymologising may put this in the same
category as spotting faces in clouds, which
in fact is an ideal activity here on a
summer's day when the sun has warmed
the grassy sandstone ledges on top of the
ridge. However, in adverse conditions the
ridge and moorland terrain becomes a far
more serious undertaking.

The walk starts from the Black Hill picnic
area, located at GR288329. To reach the
start, either take the long, high road from
Hay-on-Wye through Craswall or approach
from the south through Longtown. The
final approach takes to even narrower lanes
through Llanveynoe.

From the picnic area, cross the stile and
climb the steep bracken-covered southeast
ridge ahead which soon narrows and
passes over some sandstone outcrops. The
reward for the rapid height gain is, on a

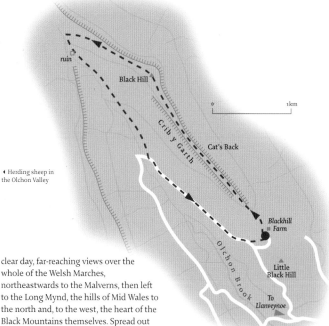

ruin

Black Hill

Crib y Garth

Cat's Back

0   1km

◄ Herding sheep in
the Olchon Valley

Blackhill
Farm

Little
Black Hill

Olchon Brook

To
Llanveynoe

clear day, far-reaching views over the whole of the Welsh Marches, northeastwards to the Malverns, then left to the Long Mynd, the hills of Mid Wales to the north and, to the west, the heart of the Black Mountains themselves. Spread out below is a patchwork of field boundaries, some of which have been in use since humans first cultivated this area. Now you can enjoy the airy walk ahead, which in 2.5km reaches the triangulation point marking the plateau-like top of Black Hill, complete with some black and boggy pools. If you are fortunate, peregrines and ring ouzels can be spotted hereabouts and on the slopes below.

The clear path wanders northwestwards over the broad heathery ridge with views ahead to the slopes leading to Hay Bluff. After 1.3km look out for a path which

switches back left, descending beside the infant Olchon Brook and past a now-ruined shepherd's stone cottage. After 500m the route enters a cleft and descends more steeply past waterfalls and rocky outcrops, down through sheep pastures and along an old walled lane to the head of the road in the valley below. Here, bear left and follow the tree-lined road for 1.75km past a number of ruined roadside cottages to reach a left turn up to Black Hill picnic area and the start.

Longtown and the Mynydd Merddin

**Distance 8km Time 2 hours 30
Terrain country lanes, riverside, field paths;
one steep ascent Map OS Explorer OL13
Access bus (441, 442) from Hereford or
Abergavenny (limited service)**

**Strong legs and some stamina are needed
for this climb up above the Upper
Monnow Valley, but the views back over
the Black Mountains are reward enough.**

Longtown is a village which, as the name
suggests, stretches itself out at the foot of
the northern scarp of the Black Mountains.
The most straightforward approach is from
Pandy on the main A465 Hereford to
Abergavenny road, but the high route from
Hay-on-Wye makes for a scenic, if longer,
run. The village itself is centred around the
meeting point of the River Monnow with
two brooks, the Escley and Olchon, while
the border with Wales runs along the

skyline ridge. Even before this was settled
by Henry VIII in the 16th century there had
been a long history of attempting to control
this 'last valley' of England. You can still see
the remains of the Norman castle at the top
end of the village.

From the centre of the village walk down
the road past The Crown pub, where a
detour left leads to the handy Village Stores,
and in 400m reach a bridge over the Olchon
Brook just above its confluence with the
River Monnow. Here, a waymarked path
turns left over stone stiles into riverside
fields for 600m with views ahead to the
scarp of the Black Mountains, soon bearing
right and then alongside the River Monnow
to the village of Clodock. Here, the Monnow
has a series of small but delightful cascades
and the church is worth a look around for its
box pews, three-tier pulpit and imposing
decalogue wall painting, while a short

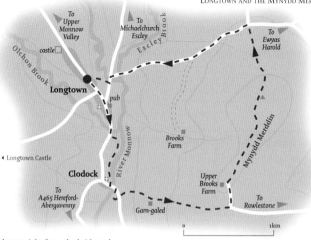

To Upper Monnow Valley
To Michaelchurch Escley
Escley Brook
To Ewyas Harold
Olchon Brook
castle
Longtown
pub
Clodock
River Monnow
Brooks Farm
Mynydd Merddin
To A465 Hereford-Abergavenny
Upper Brooks Farm
To Rowlestone
Garn-galed

◄ Longtown Castle

0   1km

detour right from the bridge takes you to The Cornewall Arms, an old parlour pub with beer, snacks and skittles.

Cross the bridge and continue along the left bank to a cottage, where the path swings left up to the lane again and across it to follow a hollow-way track up to a gate. Here, the uphill work really starts as you bear right off the track up past a house on the left and then the old barns of Garn-galed on the right, beyond which you'll need plenty of puff to follow the left-hand field edges up to and through a line of trees. The gradient now eases as the path continues up over more fields to the top of the broad ridge, where you should bear diagonally left across the top field to reach a gate onto a lane.

A left turn brings you in 350m to the end of the lane, where the route bears right and once more takes to fields just by the buildings of Upper Brooks Farm. At the

end of the second field take a track leading off left for 100m and then head diagonally across two more fields over the broad high point of the Mynydd Merddin – the triangulation point is a little way off to the right. From here there are far-reaching views up the Monnow Valley to the prominent ridge of the Cat's Back and the tops of the Black Mountains.

The route now descends along the edge of four fields to the high lane connecting Longtown to Ewyas Harold. From here, it is a simple matter of turning left for 1.75km down the hedged lane, steeply at times, back to the Monnow Valley. At the road junction just beyond the Escley Brook, turn left over the Monnow Bridge and then either keep straight on for the lower end of Longtown or turn right to follow the river path by the river and up the slope to reach the road leading to the village hall and the castle.

Ewyas Harold Common

Distance 4km Time 1 hour
Terrain footpaths, tracks, and lanes
Map OS Explorer OL13 Access bus (440,
X4) from Hereford and Abergavenny

**A short walk, but you might need to
leave plenty of time to explore this
ancient common and haven for wildlife.**

Ewyas Harold Common lies on higher
ground above the village of Ewyas Harold
and forms a boundary between the Black
Mountains and the hills of the Upper
Monnow Valley. There are over 200
commons in Herefordshire and, like
others, this one dates back many
centuries, at least to Norman times when
it was part of the county's Lord's Wood
and old manorial system. Since the 1960s
the common has been managed by local

residents and associations, who have
been concerned with improving
conditions for both wildlife and people.

It is a sensitive site, containing a wide
variety of habitats. More than 200 species
of wildflowers and ferns have been
recorded, almost 60 species of bird have
been observed, all four common reptiles
(grass-snakes, adders, common lizards
and slow worms) and all the native
amphibians (newts, frogs, toads) are
present, as well as many mammals,
butterflies, moths, and fungi. Since 2000
and the passing of the CRoW Act
(Countryside and Rights of Way Act), the
public has been granted legal access by
foot to commons. However, people still
live on the common and care should be
taken in areas undergoing repair or
felling. The suggested route takes you on
a loop to the high point of the common
and back down the southern boundary,

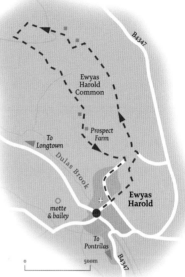

but it is easy to make detours as the mood takes you.

From the centre of the village head down School Lane to the bend and take the signed Herefordshire Trail ahead up two fields to a field-gate, beyond which a path leads up past houses to a crossroads of tracks. Here, dogleg left for 30m, then right along a pleasant woodland track which leads to a house, The Foxes, on the edge of the common.

Bear left and follow the grassy track for 600m over more open ground, which gives delightful walking and good views, across a small dip and up to a second house on the far side of the common. A dogleg left for 50m, then right takes you along a concrete track on the northern edge of the common (a relic of World War II when the common was used for military purposes) and up to some trees shading a bench at the top of Cwm Hill. These were planted in 1887 to commemorate the golden jubilee of Queen Victoria and now give an excuse to sit and absorb the impressive view to Garway Hill to the southeast, the Skirrid in the south and the Black Mountains to the west.

The onward route descends the western edge of the common for 100m, past a boundary stone, to a point level with a gate and stile in the fence. Here, swing left back across the common down a narrower path between gorse and hawthorn, crossing a track in 150m. Away to the right the tree-thicketed southern border of the common is now your guide for the next 500m – the twisting path here can become a little muddy and boggy before descending into a dip just before a house.

Here, look out for a track which goes down between a barn on the right and the house perched up on its bank on the left. At the junction with a farm track turn left and, as it bends right after 250m across a cattle grid, continue downhill into Ewyas Harold to reach the lower end of School Lane.

◀ Church of St Michael and All Angels, Ewyas Harold

Garway Hill and Jack O'Kent

Distance 9km **Time** 3-4 hours
Terrain lanes and fields; the high ground
of Garway Hill can be confusing in mist
Map OS Explorer 189 **Access** bus (X4)
from Hereford or Abergavenny to
Monmouth Cap stop, 3km west of
starting point

**Walk in the footsteps of the giant Jack
O'Kent and see seven counties from the
best viewpoint the Monnow Valley has
to offer.**

Jack O'Kent is a figure intimately
associated with Kentchurch. Some say
that he was a giant wizard in league with
the devil who had sold his soul in
exchange for supernatural powers and
that he built the bridge over the Monnow
below Grosmont in just a single night,
into the bargain short-changing the devil
out of the due payment of the first living
soul to set foot on it by throwing a bone
across, which was duly chased by a dog.
Others record the tale that he is buried in

the very walls of the church, so that being
'neither in nor out' his soul might be
confined and not snatched by the devil.
In nearby Kentchurch Park, there is even
his own oak tree, reputedly a thousand
years old and the largest in the Wye
Valley, with a girth of over 11m.

From the church 1km east of Grosmont
Bridge, head north along the road and
take the first right along a lane to Bannut
Tree Farm, with Kentchurch Park on the
right. Just beyond the farm, take the path
off right, which rises to a line of mature
oaks and alongside of former sunken
trackway into a copse to pass below Court-
a-Grove Farm. Now the route crosses a
series of six fields uphill in an easterly and
then ENE direction (in the second field bear
slightly left into the dip and through a
copse above some springs to cross a
footbridge and stile into the next field).

On reaching the road, turn right and
soon pass above a baptist chapel with
views north to Aconbury Hill. When the

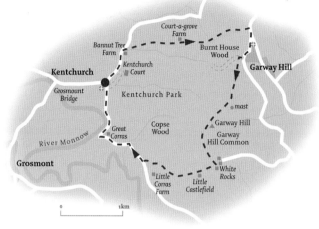

road bends back left and Garway Hill communications mast is seen ahead, turn right up a track. At the top of the rise, bear left up through woodland past the communications mast onto the open slopes of Garway Hill to its triangulation point and old pillbox. You can reputedly see seven counties on a clear day, but don't take your eye off your sandwiches, as the white mountain horses and the sheep are wise to what visitors bring with them. The horses survive on the common all year round, getting their water from nearby Black Pool, which not only mysteriously lasts all year with no visible spring but also provides a breeding ground for the rare and protected great-crested newt. The hill is a haven for wildlife and has never been ploughed. There are said to be over 70 species of bird, including skylark, song thrush and yellowhammer and it's a great habitat for butterflies.

Descend the far south side of the hill with views ahead to Dawn of the Day. On reaching the track near White Rocks – you might hear the 'hoo-hoo-hoo' or harsh 'kewick' of a thriving group of tawny owls here – turn right down past Little Castlefield, whose name recalls the former site of a Roman camp and road 1km to the southwest, near Castlefield Farm just above the Monnow. Now descend for just over 1km across fields, at first in a westerly direction, passing above a karting track and Little Corras Farm with views ahead to the Black Mountains. Then bear more to the right and aim for the left edge of the woodland ahead, before dropping down to the left to reach the road. Here, turn right and follow the lane, known now to some as the 'English Road', for a little over 1km back to Kentchurch, passing an ancient ford over the River Monnow which is still used by farm vehicles.

◀ Wild horses on Garway Hill

Index

Adstone Hill	18
All Stretton	20
Almeley	72
Apedale	22
Arrow Valley	62, 66, 70
Bishop's Castle	26
Black and White Village Trail	60, 66, 72, 74
Black Hill (Crib-y-Garth)	88
Blakemere Hill	86
Bredwardine	82
Burton Hill	74
Bury Ditches	30
Caer Caradoc Hill	20
Church Stretton Hills	6, 8, 10, 12, 14, 18
Clun	30
Clun Valley	24, 28
Colebatch Valley	26
Colva Hill	68
Craven Arms	34
Credenhill Park Wood	76
Croft Ambrey Fort	52
Dorstone	84
Downton Hill	36
Eardisland	66
Eardisley	72
Earl's Hill	10
Ewyas Harold	92
Fishpool Valley	52
Garth Hill	44
Garway Hill	94
Gladestry	68
Glynwr's Way	44
Golden Valley	78, 86
Harley's Hill	54
Hawthorn Hill	46
Hay-on-Wye	78, 80
Herefordshire Trail	50, 82, 84, 92
Hergest Ridge	62
Hopesay Hill	32
Kentchurch	94
Kington	60, 62
Knighton	42, 44
Leintwardine	36
Linley Hill	16
Llanfair Hill	28
Long Mynd, The	18
Longtown	90
Ludlow	24, 38
Lyonshall	64
Lyth Hill Country Park	8
Mary Knoll Valley	38
Merbach Hill	82
Mitchell's Fold	12
Monnow Valley	78, 90
Mortimer Trail	38, 52, 58
Mynydd Merddin	90
Newcastle	28
Newchurch	70
Norbury	16
Norton	46
Offa's Dyke	28, 44, 46, 60, 62, 64, 70
Olchon Valley	88
Onny Meadows	34
Pembridge	66
Peterchurch	86
Pontesford Hill	10
Presteigne	42, 54
Ratlinghope	18
Richards Castle	50
Rushbury	22
Shobdon Arches	56
Shrewsbury	6, 8
Shropshire Way	8, 14, 16, 18, 22, 26, 30, 32, 40
Stapeley Hill	12
Stiperstones, The	14
Stokesay Castle	34
Titley	58
Titterstone Clee Hill	40
Vagar Hill	84
Wenlock Edge	22
Weobley	60, 74
Wigmore	48
Wye Valley Walk	82